From the Soul
of
My Rubber Boots

Kimberly Dawson Hodson

Fulton Books
Meadville, PA

Published by Fulton Books 2022

ISBN 978-1-63985-898-9 (paperback)
ISBN 978-1-63985-899-6 (digital)

Printed in the United States of America

Preface

Have you ever had a "gut feeling" or a "prompting" to do something or found yourself at the right place, at the right time to somehow make a difference, help someone avoid an accident, rescue an animal, meet someone, etc.? Well, this book is just about that. The purpose of this book is to share how to really listen to your "gut feelings" or "promptings." All we have to do is "look for the bread crumbs" to find our way through this thing called life. Really *looking* and *listening* to these have saved me more times than I can count. I humbly invite you to read my book. I would love to share my true life adventures with you.

From the Soul of My Rubber Boots

Contents

How I Met Daisy

I found myself sitting in the waiting room with my late husband in the chemotherapy department. He had been diagnosed with nasopharyngeal cancer and had been receiving extensive chemotherapy and radiation treatments for six months. We were waiting for the appointment that follows after all the chemo and radiation treatments are completed. This is the appointment that lets you know if it worked—if the cancer was gone or not. I was trying not to worry and trust God. I had been in constant prayer, asking and begging God to heal him. For the past six months, I had watched my late husband become so skinny. He had lost over one hundred pounds.

I knew we were getting to a dangerously scary place. Every time we walked into the chemotherapy and radiation department, I asked God to help me. The waiting rooms were full to overflowing with cancer patients. There were so many of them. I had no idea that so many people had cancer. The waiting room was so heavy with emotion.

My late husband seemed to be stronger than me. He liked to visit with the other patients and to talk to them about hope and about God. He felt confident about God healing him and always said that either way, he was a winner! He knew where he was going if it was his turn to be called home.

As we waited for what seemed like forever, we were finally called back to one of the examination rooms to see the doctor. More waiting. Finally, the doctor came in.

He looked at my husband and said, "You already know what I am going to say, don't you?"

My late husband smiled.

The doctor said, "You are cancer-free!"

My late husband shook his hand and said, "I knew God would take care of me."

What? I thought. *Did I hear correctly?*

You see, the doctors had taken away all hope for healing and had given him a short time to live.

I hugged my late husband so tightly and said, "God saved you! He has great purpose for you!"

He just said, "Oh yeah, I know. He already told me."

On the drive home, I had so much peace and joy.

My late husband said, "Hey! Let's get that milking goat that you always wanted!"

What? I was shocked. You see, for as long as I could remember, I had always wanted to have a milking goat to milk and to make cheese and yogurt.

It was too easy. I found a lady who had a milking goat for sale, and she had already trained her. She was even willing to teach me! I had to go check out this goat for myself. As the lady pointed the goat out, I leaned forward to say hi, and she came right up to me and put her nose next to mine! It was love at first sight! I named her Daisy.

I brought her home, and we began our adventure! I began to milk her every morning and every night just as the lady instructed. I was getting better each time. I had successfully milked her three days in a row. It had been four days since we got the amazing news that my late husband was healed from cancer. I was feeling so happy and hopeful about everything.

I had no idea what was about to come next.

My late husband called me as I was driving home from work and said, "Come home soon. Something has happened."

He wouldn't tell me what it was on the phone. My heart sank again. Once again, I had that same feeling. The feeling that I thought I had gotten rid of.

"Oh, God, not again," I said.

As I got home, I saw my late husband standing in the driveway with tears rolling down his cheeks. I didn't want to get out of the car, but I knew I had to.

Silently, I prayed, "Please, God, help me!"

As I slowly got out of the car, he told me that my little brother, Mark, had passed away.

How could that possibly be true? I thought. *I had just talked to him about two hours ago.*

He had been found at home on his bed from an apparent asthma attack. My legs became so weak they could not hold me up. My whole body went limp, and I fell forward as my late husband caught me. My heart literally felt like it had been stabbed. There are no words to describe the severe pain of sudden loss. It is the worst pain I have ever felt. I loved Mark so much. We used to always say, "Thank goodness we have each other!" We understood each other like no one else did.

I took to my bed. I couldn't work. I couldn't do anything. I realized that I had to milk Daisy.

"Oh no! Daisy needs me!"

If I didn't milk her, she would be in severe pain. Somehow, I found the strength to go outside and milk Daisy. I grabbed my stainless steel milking bucket and walked to the back of the property. As I got her up on the milking stand, she would put her head on my shoulder. I would put the bucket in place and begin milking. As I started milking, I would begin to cry. I would cry and cry and cry and I would ask God, "Where is Mark?" Daisy would keep her head on my shoulder, and sometimes she would put her cheek next to mine or put her nose next to my nose, and she would stay very still. I would lean my head against hers, and she let me cry on her for as long as I needed to. I did this every morning and every night for weeks. I would ask God the same thing, "Where is Mark?" I felt so alone, and I missed him so much that it hurt. Each time I finished, I ended up with a full bucket of milk, and my tears would be gone. For that moment, I would have a little peace. Each time, the peace would last a bit longer. Each day, I would ask God the same thing, "Where is Mark?"

One day, I could hear in my heart, "I have Mark and he is good! I have him in my arms! And I am with you too! You are not alone, and you have great purpose."

Me? Great purpose? I thought.

He must have the wrong person. I could barely get through each day. I had just come through the most unbelievable roller-coaster ride with the healing of my late husband's cancer then the sudden death of my brother. It was more than I could bear.

I continued to milk Daisy every morning and every night for months. I began to feel God with me when I was milking her, and the tears finally began to slow down. I felt so much peace when I was milking her, and I knew that God had given her to me and at the exact time that I would need her the most. He used Daisy to reach me and to remind me that He was with me and to comfort me about Mark. From the outside, it just looked like I was milking a goat to make cheese or yogurt like most people do who live on farms. It was so much more than that. To me, it was supernatural.

The saying that God works in mysterious ways is an understatement. God knew my dream of having my own milking goat, and He used this to help reach me, help heal me, and bring me to a place of peace. I finally was able to say that I know Mark was with God and that I know I will see him again. God is in control of life and death, and I am so thankful that this life is not all there is.

Since then, I have been prompted to share this story about Daisy and losing my brother with many people who have also lost a loved one to a sudden death. I have seen so many people helped by my story; that is truly amazing. My story comforts people, and I know that it helps them the same way that it helped me. God is using me to reach others who are in pain too. I guess He does have great purpose for me. I also tell others that God has great purpose for them too.

Which Came First, the Chicken or the Egg?

"Why chickens?" people would ask when I described all the animals that I wanted to have on my farm and ultimately use as therapy animals. Most people wouldn't choose chickens for pets because they can be noisy, smelly, and ruin your vegetable gardens. I have heard this over and over, and yet I continue to be drawn to them and not just for their amazing organic eggs.

I think I became fonder of them after my brother Mark passed away. You see, I had been babysitting his four chickens right before he died. After his passing, they somehow got out of their cage and began just running around loose on our farm. I didn't have the energy or the wherewithal to even try to catch them. The grief of losing my little brother was almost more than I could take, and I could just barely make it through each day. All I could do was to pray that God would keep them safe. I knew my brother had named each one of his chickens after our grandmother "Ruth," my great-grandmother "Granny," and two great aunts, "Aunt Sissy" and "Aunt Jessie."

On one very sad day, when I just couldn't stop crying about my brother, I noticed that his chicken (the one named Ruth) had laid a blue egg. I thought it was nice but didn't think much of it. Then as time went on, it became quite clear that each time I would cry or ask "Mark, where are you?" a blue egg would just *show up* in the strangest places. Each time, I would pick up the blue eggs and gently carry them into the house smiling and thinking of Mark. I started

5

to pay more attention to the arrival of these blue eggs. I became keenly aware of the timing. They would always arrive when I would be especially sad or down about Mark. Sometimes, a month would go by before I would see a blue egg. I would find one each and every time just when I really needed it and when I was feeling the saddest.

One day, Ruth started following me all around the yard. Often, she would frequently come up next to me and crawl into my lap. I like to sit on a small stool near the barn, so I can be with all of my farm animals. She started to let me gently rub her back and wings. Her feathers were so soft. Ruth would sit very still, and I would talk to her. She seemed to love sitting with me. I grew very attached to her and realized what a kind and gentle spirit she had. I began to wonder if any of her blue eggs were fertile.

What if she had babies? I thought.

I couldn't get that notion out of my head. I really wanted to know more about hatching eggs. I started watching videos and reading as much as I could. I continued to think about how I have secretly wanted to see a baby chick actually hatch from its egg for as long as I can remember. What a miraculous thing that would be! I have quite a few laying hens and a few roosters that roam free around my farm, and we periodically get new baby chicks that hatch out in the pasture.

One afternoon as I was out feeding all the animals, I couldn't help but notice that Ruth was sitting on a pile of eggs! As I threw the chicken feed out for all of the chickens, she actually got up and left her eggs to go eat with the others. I couldn't seem to take my eyes off the eggs. I just had to pick one of them up. They were so beautiful with such different colors! Some were blue and brown, and some were even spotted with white and beige. I grabbed a brown one. As I held it in my right hand, I couldn't help but notice it was surprisingly warm and slightly heavy. It was heavier than I thought it would be.

As I held it, I remember thinking, *Oh, how I wish I could see this egg hatch.*

I intended to put it back on the pile of eggs, but I couldn't help but hesitate.

Why was I hesitating? I wondered.

I had a crazy thought! I wanted to keep it.

Could I? I thought.

Why couldn't I just hatch it myself? Others have done it. But how could I do it? I had the craziest idea! I will take it with me and use body heat to hatch it. I knew just the place to put it. Right next to my heart. As I walked back into the house, I gently placed her there. I had already identified the egg as a girl.

I walked into the bedroom and sat down next to my late husband. I was thinking about how to tell him about this crazy harebrained idea. He was kind of used to me coming up with crazy ideas. Usually, when I came up with one, I would jump right in with both feet. When I get fun ideas, I don't like to wait. I especially did not want to wait with this one, and I knew that I couldn't wait because the egg had to stay warm.

What's the harm? I thought.

The question was how would I tell my family? Of all the crazy ideas I have had, this one definitely was one of the craziest! As I sat down with my late husband and kids, I proceeded to tell them about the egg that I found, then I told them that I was going to try to hatch it on my own.

"How?" my son asked as he was half focused on his TV show.

"Well," I said, "I will place it next to my heart."

"What!" he said.

All I could hear after that was insatiable laughter from each one of them. They laughed and laughed and laughed. I knew it was a crazy idea, but I was compelled to try it. I had always wanted to see an egg hatch, and here was my chance. I begged my family not to tell anyone because it was such an absurd idea. They quickly agreed. They didn't want anyone to know either!

I put it next to my heart and kept it there all the time. I slept with it, and I took it with me to work. I learned how to move carefully so as not to break the egg. I even learned how to bend over and pick things up off the floor without loosening it. Sleeping was challenging because I was so afraid of rolling over and breaking her. I woke up a lot during the night to check on her. It reminded me of when our children were newborn babies, and we never slept well because we were up and down all night, checking on them constantly. I learned to sleep only on my back for a while. I found a few problems though, like what to do with her when I took a shower.

I asked my late husband to hold her next to his heart. He was usually a good sport even when he really didn't want to do something. I couldn't help but smile when I would come out of the shower and see him sitting there on the couch holding the egg against his heart while watching his favorite TV show. I knew he definitely loved me.

One day when I was at work, I met someone who was very sad and was recovering from a tragic car accident. She was really having a bad day and kept crying about how she almost died and was so scared to ever get into a car again. She also cried about the other person who was with her that died in the accident and that she felt to blame because she was the driver. She had broken her legs so badly that the doctors didn't think she would ever walk again. Her life had truly been changed in one single moment. She really needed some uplifting. I was her occupational therapist, and it was my job to help rehabilitate her and help her to get stronger, so she could return home, independent with her daily life. I felt prompted to tell her about the egg, but I didn't want to tell her. I just knew she would think I was crazy. I kept getting the prompting over and over. I knew I should tell her. But how?

I began to tell her about my dream of hatching an egg and that I had found an egg in my yard. She seemed excited and shared that she used to raise chickens and loved having them as pets. I wanted to stop right there, but I continued to have the prompting to share the whole story.

Oh boy! I thought. *Here goes nothing!*

I told her that I decided to use my own body heat to hatch it.

She asked, "How would you do that? Where would you put it?"

"Well," I said softly with a very long pause, "I put it right next to my heart."

Her eyes got as big as saucers, and she exclaimed, "Is it with you now?"

I quietly said yes, kind of afraid of what she would think.

She burst into the loudest laughter! She laughed and then laughed some more! Her whole countenance changed. She smiled and energetically began to talk about her fun memories of living on a farm as a child and told me all about her pet chickens, their names, and how they would follow her all around the yard and sit on her lap. She thanked me for helping her feel happy and to get her mind off her sad situation.

I smiled and said, "Please don't ever tell anyone about this! They will think I am crazy!"

No one at my job knew what I was doing, and I wanted to keep it that way. I remember leaving her room thinking how happy I was that my crazy story could help her. I knew deep in my heart that God had prompted me to share this. I went to work knowing that I would not tell anyone about what I was doing. God had other plans.

I continued on with this daily routine with the egg for several weeks. I became so fond of her. I loved knowing she was with me everywhere I went. I found myself talking to her. At times, I would reach up and place my hand on her and softly tell her that I loved her. From the moment she had been placed next to my heart, I was never alone. Even when I was in important staff meetings, I felt the comfort of having her with me. I did, however, pray that she wouldn't hatch inside the meetings! That would have been an interesting situation! I had visions of this precious little one someday soon just popping out of her egg! I had been researching eggs hatching, and I knew it would take twenty-one days before it hatched. The time was getting close. I got her little basket ready and put a soft fluffy blanket inside and placed it on my bedside table right next to me. Day twenty-one came and went. I thought maybe I had miscounted the days.

I began to hope that I miscounted. I woke up one morning with such a sad feeling.

Could something be wrong with her? I thought.

I had such great plans for this little one. She and I were going to be inseparable. I had already been thinking of names. Throughout the day, I couldn't get rid of the sad feeling and the thought that something might be wrong. I couldn't believe how sad I was. As much as I didn't want to admit it, I knew that this little egg that I had been loving and caring for, carrying around with me day and night, sleeping lightly not to cause harm, talking to and telling her I loved her was no longer a viable egg. I came home from work and walked to the back of the property. I was so sad. I couldn't believe how sad I was actually feeling. I felt as if I had lost her, but I hadn't even gotten to know her. I had gotten so attached.

I found a shady spot under the grapefruit tree. As I knelt down, I couldn't hold back the tears. I buried her right there. I had to say goodbye, but I didn't want to. I told God that I was sorry that I had taken the egg away from her mother just so I could try to hatch her and keep her for myself. I had never really told anyone how much I had dreamed of actually seeing a baby chick hatch from its egg. Only God knew. As I walked back to the house, I was already missing her being next to my heart.

Several weeks went by as I tried to adjust to not having her.

One day, when I was outside feeding the chickens again, I saw another pile of eggs!

"No," I told myself. *Never again! Just walk away!*

I tried to walk away, but I did want to look at them. I went closer and noticed that there were fifteen beautiful blue and brown and white eggs. I felt a gentle prompting to pick two of them up. At first, I didn't want to, but it was a peaceful prompting, and I really missed holding a baby chicken egg. Before I knew it, I was holding two of them. But I told myself I will not try to take them this time. I will put them back to be with their mother. I had a blue egg in one hand and a brown egg in the other. They were so warm and clean and a little heavy. Right at that moment, I noticed that something began to happen. They started to shake and move back and forth a little.

"Could it be!"

The eggs started to get small cracks in them!

This cannot be happening! I thought.

I stood there in the middle of the farm holding these eggs that were actually hatching right in my hands. I was so full of emotion that I could hardly contain myself. I yelled for my daughter. She came running to me, and she and I stood there and watched. This was truly remarkable. Two beautiful baby chicks emerged right in my hands! We couldn't stop smiling. I took them inside and placed them in the basket that I had prepared for the first egg. I had a warming light already set up, and I gently placed them inside. They were precious and were already walking around and chirping. As I sat on the side of my bed, I looked at them in such amazement.

How? I thought. *What had made me pick up the eggs again? What if I hadn't? I would have missed out on such a miracle.*

Deep in my heart, I remembered that one of my greatest wishes was to see a baby chick actually hatch from its egg. I had tried to force it on my own. Even though I had done everything with good intention with the first egg, it had not been meant to be. But when I followed the prompting, everything fell right into place. Only God had known of my secret dream. Then I thought of the timing of it all. Right when I picked up the eggs, they began to hatch. How had I been standing right next to the pile of eggs, and what if I didn't follow the prompting to actually pick them up again? If I hadn't paid attention to these promptings that I know were from God, I would have missed out on one of the most amazing miracles. It was as if I could hear God say in my heart, "If you will wait on Me, we can do things together, and you will see amazing blessings and miracles! I hear your dreams! If you try it on your own, you will only be forcing things to happen and it's not in My timing."

From then on, the two little baby chicks and I were inseparable. I put them in a little pouch, and I took them everywhere. They would ride around on my shoulders, and they slept with me nuzzled underneath my chin. Once in a while, they would sneak over and sleep on my late husband's chest. This happiness cannot be put into words.

Thank you, God, for this gift. I pray that I can remember this story and the importance of listening for God's promptings.

How I Got Donald

Life had suddenly become overwhelming and chaotic. My late husband was finishing up his six months of radiation and chemotherapy, and I was just trying to take care of all of the day-to-day responsibilities as well as keeping everyone's spirits up. We had taken our two beloved horses to stay in a pasture while my late husband was getting treatments because we had a lot of medical bills, and we couldn't afford to buy them horse food. We tried to visit them when we could, but the visits were rare. The owner of the property put a goat in there with our horses. They all seemed to get along and actually they became very close. The goat had to be right next to the horses. I had heard that goats make good companions for horses and that they used goats to comfort even racehorses. Each time we had to leave from a visit, I felt really sad and knew the horses felt the same. Knowing that the goat was with them gave me a little peace that they had a friend.

The owner of the property called one day and said that he had gotten into some trouble with some bad people, and he was headed for jail! He said we better get the horses out of the property as soon as possible because he didn't think the horses would be safe. He also said the bad guys might try to take the horses and sell them for money.

What! How is this even happening? I thought.

It felt like a nightmare. I told my late husband, and he said he would just go over and get them. I couldn't even take off work to help him. He, my son, and my daughter hooked up the horse trailer and headed straight for the pasture. I was at work, and I couldn't stop feeling worried and afraid.

After what seemed like hours, my late husband called and said, "Well, I have some good news and some interesting news."

I just wanted to know that the horses were safe and out of that pasture, but I knew something must have happened.

So I closed my eyes and took a deep breath and said, "Okay, tell me."

He said, "You remember that goat that was stuck to the horses? Well, as we were driving away with the horses in the trailer, he kept jumping the fence and running down the road after us."

He explained that they had to take the goat back four times and put him in the pasture, and each time, he jumped the fence and ran after them down the road. And on the last time, he almost got hit by a car. They finally just put him in the trailer with the horses and headed home. It was either bring him home or let him get lost or hit by a car. I could not believe what I was hearing.

He called the owner and told him what happened, and the owner said, "Can you keep him please? I am afraid the bad guys will hurt him or even try to eat him."

My late husband was tolerant of my crazy passion for animals, but this was such a kind and amazing gesture. I was thankful that he had so much compassion for this goat.

Now what will we do with him? I thought.

This goat was rather large with big horns, and one horn that looked like he had been injured because it was broken in half. I couldn't wait to get home to see all of this. Work that day seemed to drag on forever! When I finally got home, I could see the horses and the goat as I drove up the driveway. They were still all together. I went to them and hugged the horses and welcomed them home and told them I loved and missed them. They were happy to be home. I could feel it. The goat came right up to me and stared straight into my eyes. As I reached out to pet his head, he dropped his head a little and walked a little closer to me. He let me scratch his back as he stood very close. I knew I had made a friend. I also knew he was thankful to be here with us and the horses. From that day on, the three of them stayed together and ran all over the property together. We decided to name him Donald.

I could feel something different with Donald. It was like I could feel his spirit. Each time I went outside, he came straight to me and pressed against my side as if to ask for a good head and back scratch. I knew he loved me. I could sense it. I certainly loved him. He was one of us now.

Soon after he joined our family, we had a family tragedy. My brother had a sudden death from an asthma attack. I was devastated. I could not contain my grief. I took to my bed, and I only got up to milk Daisy, my other goat. The rest of the time, I tried to sleep away my sadness. I started to get up late at night, around 3:00 a.m., and I would go sit outside on the back deck and just sit. I would quietly cry out to God and ask Him why this had happened and where was my brother. Donald began to come near me, and he would sit right next to me. He was so big that when he sat down next to me, his head was next to my head.

One night, I was so sad, I could not hold back the tears. He leaned over and placed his right cheek next to my left cheek, and his nose was right next to my nose. He sat very still and did not move. I placed my arm around him, and I closed my eyes. His breath was so sweet, and his breathing became slow and steady; and I knew at that moment that he could feel my pain and sadness and that he wanted to make me feel better. We sat like this many late nights together.

Each time, my tears were less, and I began to feel peace little by little. I could hear in my heart that it was going to be okay.

It may seem like we saved this broken-horned lonely goat, but I knew that it was just the opposite. We may have given him a home, but he helped to save me. I knew that God had brought him to me and used him to help me through my sadness. The love I felt from Donald was surely supernatural. It transcended through him to me when I needed it most.

As I reflect back, I know that God and His angels were with me. He heard my crying, and He used Donald to reach me. I know that this was God's way of letting me know that I am not alone and that He is here. Right here.

There are so many times that God tries to talk with us, to let us know that He loves us. We can begin to hear Him if we will only listen. His clues and signs are all around us. I wanted to be able to see the clues and signs more clearly. It reminds me of the scripture Deuteronomy 31:8, "The Lord Himself goes before you and will be with you; He will never leave you nor forsake you. Do not be afraid; do not be discouraged."

Annabelle, Sophie, Olive, and Renée

I am not sure what is cuter than little miniature milking goats. My four little females sure were the most adorable little ones that I had ever seen. Every day, I couldn't wait to go outside to be with them.

They were all pregnant and all were very close to their due dates for giving birth. I knew all of the signs of labor. I meticulously checked each one of them. They were ready. I could feel that the day was so very close. I found my foldable reclining beach chair and placed it inside their birthing pen. I was not going to miss any of it. I had secretly been asking God, "Please let me be there when they give birth."

As I got my pillow and blanket, I entered their pen and patted each one on the head and said, "I am here, girls. Don't worry. Everything will be okay."

I wasn't really sure if everything would be okay, but I wanted to make everything okay. I had raised each one from birth and I loved them, and they loved me. Annabelle and Sophie were sisters, and Olive and Renée were Annabelle's daughters. As I laid on the beach chair, Annabelle jumped up on my chair and settled next to my feet, and Renee laid next to my head on my pillow. They were small enough to fit comfortably next to me. Sophie and Olive pawed themselves a bed in the soft straw that I had made for them. Everyone put their heads down as if to go to sleep for the night. I did the same. After what seemed like minutes of being asleep, I woke up to whimpering or crying sounds.

The girls had gotten down from my beach chair and all of them were walking around as if they were pacing. *Oh boy!* I knew that this was a sign. I quickly checked each one, and Annabelle began to give birth! The baby came out so fast! Thankfully, I remembered to bring out old towels. The baby was precious. I wiped its nose and mouth, and Annabelle began to clean her, being the good mother that she is. Before I could even finish, out came another one! I quickly started to clean the next one too, making sure that they both were breathing, and soon they both began to cry. She had a boy and a girl.

Sophie was next. She gave birth quickly to one boy, and I jumped to clean his nose and mouth too. He was the first to try to nurse, trying to stand on his four little shaking legs. Within twenty minutes, Olive gave birth to a tiny, little girl. I was in a rhythm, and I raced to clean her little nose and mouth. All the babies were wiggly and crying and trying to stand up.

It was Renée's turn. I kept my eyes on her. Within an hour, she gave birth to a tiny, little boy. I grabbed the last clean towel and started to clean his nose and mouth. Something was different with this one. He wasn't wiggling like the others. I rubbed his little body to try to wake him up. He wasn't breathing. I tried so hard to get him to start breathing. Renée tried to clean him, and she began to lick him all over his face. She began to nudge him with her nose. He felt limp in my arms. I felt so sick in my stomach. I kept trying so hard to revive him. I finally laid him down gently on the towel. Renée kept cleaning him while the other three were finally getting the hang of nursing their babies. As I sat there right in the middle of all of them, I felt so many emotions. The sadness for Renee was overwhelming.

After a little while, Annabelle, Sophie, and Olive had made a little bed to sit with their babies all cuddled up against each of them. Renée looked at me. I could only imagine what she was thinking or feeling.

I wrapped her baby up in the towel with his little head resting in my hand. She started to make a whimpering sound, then she walked over to the farthest place in the pen and sat down and put her head down. This was probably one of the saddest moments that I could ever remember.

As Renée sat alone, the others all looked up and gazed over at her little dead baby. What happened next was unbelievable. Annabelle, Sophie, and Olive each stood up and walked toward the little baby. They stood in sort of a line and then Annabelle actually walked up to the baby, dropped her head, and placed her nose against him for just a moment. Then she walked back toward her own two little babies. Sophie and Olive followed Annabelle and each one went up to the baby and placed their noses against him one after another as if to kiss the baby goodbye and "pay their respects."

I could not believe what I was seeing. Did these little goats have the ability to sense or feel each other's pain or loss? If I had stayed in the house, not only would I have missed the amazing births, but most importantly, I would have missed this display of love and compassion from these little farm animals. An amazing miracle happened right in front of my eyes, and I could have so easily missed it.

As the new little babies grew, they began to run and play, and they were thriving. They had learned how to nurse from their own mothers very well. They all stayed together including Renée. While all the others were nursing their babies, I was milking Renée to relieve her of her painfully engorged udders. As she stood in the milking stand, I could sense her sadness as she watched the others actually nursing their babies. Not too long after this, I was sitting out in the pasture with all of them and their playful little babies. I couldn't help but notice Annabelle. She began to stand very close to Renée. All of a sudden, she nudged her little boy baby toward Renée.

What was she doing? I thought.

She continued to do this several times. Then all of a sudden, the little baby boy tried to nurse Renée! He quickly latched onto to her and began nursing! When baby goats nurse they make the cutest little sounds, and he began to make these.

Could it be? I thought.

I sat with them for a while and this little boy began to go back and forth, nursing between Annabelle and Renée. It seemed as if Annabelle could feel Renée's pain so much that she decided to share her baby. What a display of love.

Again, I thought, *I could have so easily missed this!*

These animals have demonstrated such love. I felt so blessed to have been allowed to see this. After a while, Renee seemed to be happy to be able to nurse a baby too, and all the babies began to grow and flourish.

I spent most of my afternoons sitting in my beach chair in the middle of the pasture with them. I would frequently think of how I could have so easily missed seeing all of the amazing miracles and these little ones if I hadn't followed the *prompting* to go outside and sit with them. I could have easily missed all of it if I had been focusing on my busy day-to-day life. I was so thankful that I had felt the *promptings*. I wanted to learn how to hear and see them more.

Three Hundred Dollars

- - - - - - -

I found myself sitting alone at the kitchen table on one very warm Sunday afternoon. I was trying to desperately pay the bills. This was a big feat. You see, my late husband had been out of work for almost two years, and there really was not enough money to pay our basic bills. One month I would pay some, and then the next month I would pay others. I was behind on them all.

My late husband had a good job as a police officer, but he had been involved in an incident which involved the kidnapping of an elderly couple and the perpetrator had used a sawed-off shotgun to hold them hostage. My late husband had one chance to save them as well as the other officers. He took the shot. He saved them and his fellow officers, and the bad guy did not even die from the bullet wound. The police department supported my husband's actions, however they put him on leave without pay and told him to "take some time" due to possible "PTSD."

I remember getting his phone call that day when he said, "Something has happened. I have shot someone in the line of duty. I love you and I am sorry. Our lives will never be the same."

As I hung up the phone, I asked God to not let the man die, and if He would spare his life, I would live with whatever happened after that. I knew my late husband would not be able to bear the thought of knowing that he had killed someone. The journey after the shooting was a long one. We all struggled. My late husband struggled with finding himself again and coming to terms with what had actually happened. The kids and I were trying to cope with the changes with everything else. This included never having enough money for anything. One month, we had to eat chicken noodle soup for every meal.

Someone had given us a case of that soup, and we couldn't afford to eat anything else.

In one moment, our lives had changed completely. I tried to keep things in the family as "normal" as I could, taking the kids to their activities and school functions and trying to keep everyone's spirits up. It was hard to do this on this particular day. I couldn't even keep my own spirits up. I was facing the truth of no money. We had been given the cancellation notice from the electric company. I would have to pay three hundred dollars by the next day, or our electricity would be turned off. I only had enough money to pay that or pay for food and gas to get to work and take the kids to school. I couldn't pay both.

Which one do I pay? What should I do? I thought.

I asked my late husband, but he was having an especially hard day, and he said, "I really don't know. I am sure you will make the right decision."

I didn't know what to do to make the right decision. I couldn't make any decision. I felt so alone. I didn't tell anyone about our dilemma. Maybe I was embarrassed, or maybe I was just trying to figure out how to keep my head above water; but no one knew about the threat of losing electricity. I began to beg God for help. I just kept saying, "Please, God, help me. Please, God, help me!" I went outside in the pasture to be with my animals as I usually did on Sunday afternoons. Being with the animals was where I found my peace. I really felt God's presence there. Each Sunday afternoon was my time to be with them.

As I came back into the house, I heard the dogs barking, and I knew the sound of their barks meant someone was in front of the house. I stepped out of the front door and noticed a man standing at the gate. I asked him if I could help him.

He said, "God asked me to give you this," as he handed me a white envelope.

I automatically reached and took the envelope. As I looked down at the envelope, I began to open it. I couldn't believe my eyes! Inside the envelope were three one-hundred-dollar bills! I looked back at the man, and he was gone. He was completely gone. He was nowhere! I looked up and down the road and there was no sign of him.

Who was he? Where in the world did he go? I thought. *How did he know the exact amount of money that I needed? I had not told anyone.*

I stood in the middle of the driveway holding the envelope with the money with my mouth wide open.

After I was able to get some kind of composure, I went back inside. I started to tell my husband, but he was watching a football game. I went to tell my kids what had happened, but they were playing with their toys, and they really had no idea how bad our money situation had become. I went into the bedroom and just fell face-first onto the bed. I couldn't believe what had just happened. I could feel in my heart that God was saying, "This blessing was just for you so that you will know, without a doubt, that I hear your prayers and you are not alone. I am with you." All I could do was thank God over and over as I felt so much peace in my heart. God truly had heard my prayer begging for help. I still didn't know who in the world that man was. Was he an angel or just a kind stranger that God had asked to help me? It had happened so fast that I could not even remember what he had looked like.

Thirteen years later, I met a very nice lady at work who was one of my patients. I work as an occupational therapist. Her son brought her in twice a week for therapy. Each time he would bring her in, the three of us would often talk and laugh about silly everyday things all the while she was getting stronger with her therapy. She had continued to come for therapy for about three months, and her therapy was almost over with me.

One Sunday afternoon, as usual, I found myself outside in the pasture. I was just walking around, enjoying the goats and my old ranch horse. All of a sudden, I heard something so loud in my heart it could have been audible, but I knew it couldn't be!

I heard, "The man that gave you the three hundred dollars is your patient's son!"

No way! No way! *No way!* I absolutely couldn't believe it.

Then I heard in my heart, "Ask him."

"No," I said aloud.

I did not and would not and could not ask him. He would think I was totally insane. I continued to have this internal discussion with myself and with God. I just could not see how this could be true. I had been with him and his mother for three months. We became friends. We laughed together and his mother had made so much progress, and it was time for her therapy to end soon. What would he think if I asked him such a crazy question?

The next day, I found myself in the therapy room with him and his mother. I continued to feel the prompting to ask him. I so did not want to. I really felt the strong prompting to go ahead and ask him.

I finally said, "Okay, God, I will do as you want, and I will ask."

I mustered up the courage to start. I said, "Can I ask you a question?"

"Of course," he said.

I hemmed and hawed, stuttering and pausing. I finally just said very quickly, "Is there any chance that you went to a house thirteen years ago and gave a lady three hundred dollars?"

There, I said it. I let out a long sigh and waited. I didn't even want to look at him. After a long pause, I just had to look up at him because he didn't say anything.

Then he got a peaceful look on his face and said, "Well, you know, the right hand is not supposed to tell the left hand what he is doing"

"What!"

It was a good thing I was sitting down because I probably would have fainted from shock. How in the world? I knew that saying. It was from the Bible. It meant that when you do something kind for someone, you should not tell anyone or brag about it. It is to be done in secret for God's glory.

I didn't know what to do or say next. I explained that I had felt a prompting from God to ask him. He just smiled and said he had been prompted from God to give it. I would never in a million years have thought to ask him that question. I truly had a prompting from

God when I was out in the pasture. It had to be God talking to me. There is no doubt in my mind that God had spoken to me that day. I knew that it was God reminding me again that He hears my prayers and is with me guiding and directing me. If only I would pay more attention to His clues and promptings, I could hear Him even more. I cannot express the peace that I felt when I truly knew that God Himself had heard my prayers and had talked to me. He had orchestrated this whole scenario to ensure that there could be no doubt that it was Him! What if I had refused to follow the prompting to ask the question? What if I had chosen to just go about my day as I usually did, focusing only on the worldly distractions and responsibilities? I would have missed the most amazing miracle that He created just for me. Does He really love me that much to go to such unusual circumstances to prove it?

I am beginning to believe that He does.

The Bees

- - - ● - - - ●

Have you ever found yourself in a situation that you truly felt that you did not have the strength to overcome? Where it felt that it was too much to take, and you had no idea how or what to do?

Well, this type of situation fell upon me. It was an ordinary day. I was busy helping my daughter get ready for her prom. It was a very warm day in April, and the excitement of getting hair and nails done, pressing last-minute wrinkles out of the prom dress, and keeping makeup from melting so the pictures turned out beautiful was my focus. I got a phone call in the middle of all of this.

It was a guy stating, "I can only come today to remove your beehive. Take it or leave it."

I had forgotten that I called for a beehive removal because we had found a very large beehive in the barn. Bees had started a small swarm within the barn, and I absolutely had to get them removed within the next week. We were going on vacation the following week, and my neighbor was going to come over to feed the animals. He was terrified of bees.

Today? I thought.

We had to leave soon to go take pictures for the prom! No one would even be home. I had a bad feeling in my stomach, but I was distracted. I really didn't think I had a choice. I told him to come on over. As we began loading up our daughter in her long flowing prom dress into the car, guarding her hair from the wind, trying not to get any part of her messy, up drove the bee guy. He pulled into the driveway in his small, blue Datsun pickup truck, driving a bit too fast for me. Again, I had that same bad feeling.

I walked him over to the barn to show him the beehive, which was partially hidden in the double wall in the back. I especially wanted him to know about all of our animals, including five miniature goats, three large goats, one sheep, two horses, and a dozen chickens. Each one of these animals has a special story of how they came to live with us. I tried to tell this guy how important my beloved animals were and asked him to be very careful. He was hardly listening to me as he began knocking on the wall of the barn to begin his job to remove the bees.

I heard my family yelling, "Let's go! We will be late!"

I reluctantly told the guy that I was leaving. My neighbor was with me, and he said he would "keep an eye on things." Knowing how much I love all of the animals, I knew my daughter was my priority. I said a little prayer to God, asking Him to please protect everyone on the farm. They are my babies too. Even though I had just prayed, I felt worried. I tried to hide it from everyone. I wanted this prom to be wonderful. My kids had just come through a very challenging year. My late husband had just completed six months of intense chemo and radiation treatments for terminal cancer and was just given the "all clear." My kids saw their father lose over one hundred pounds and suffer with the side effects of these treatments. They chose to give up a lot of school activities because of this. They wanted to be with their dad. I wanted her to feel like a regular teenager today and enjoy her prom. I just couldn't let her see my concern, or she would not be able to relax and enjoy it.

I put on a big smile as we all jumped out of the car to take pictures of her and her date in a tropical botanical garden. Everything went just as planned and on schedule until I got another phone call. I was reluctant to even answer the phone. I didn't want my daughter to think I was putting anything priority over her special event. I knew I needed to answer it. It was our neighbor.

He said, "Something has gone terribly wrong! What should I do?"

He explained that the bee guy had just began ripping the back of the barn apart and a massive swarm of bees came flying out. The bee guy kept yelling, "Get the animals out!" My neighbor tried to get them out, but the swarm was too big. The bee guy said the hive was at least ten feet in height, and he had never seen one that big! He kept loading up huge buckets and buckets of honey.

As he began to drive away, he yelled, "If the animals stop breathing, just call the vet!"

The swarm was huge! The animals were running around in circles, running into each other, and crying and screaming. Most of the bees were all around the animals, but he saw a swarm follow the bee guy's truck that looked like a dark cloud! It followed him down the driveway and out onto the road! My neighbor tried to get the water hose to spray the animals, but he ended up getting stung multiple times and had to give up.

Again, he said, "What should I do?"

I told him thank you and to take care of his beestings and that I would get home as fast as I could.

My heart stopped. I remembered knowing something didn't feel right. Again, I prayed. This time, my prayer was something like this: "Please, God, please! Help them and help me know what to do!" I was helpless. I continued to pray constantly inside while continuing to smile and take prom pictures. I didn't want to tell anyone yet. Not until everyone was on their way to the prom. I just continued to hold my breath and smile and especially pray.

After what seemed like hours, everyone headed to the prom, and it was time for all of us to leave the botanical gardens. My late husband and son were in one car, and they were headed off to the hardware store to pick up random supplies. My mom was with me, and we were going to head home. I whispered to my late husband that there was a problem with the bees and that I was headed home. I didn't want him to stress out either, so I didn't give him all the critical details.

As my mom and I got into the car, I said, "Um..."

She knew something was wrong. She asked, "What's wrong? I know every time you start out a sentence with 'Um,' something is wrong."

I wanted to hide it from her too, but I couldn't. So I told her everything I could remember. I told her I would drop her off at her house first.

"No way! I am coming with you!"

How could I rescue all the animals while protecting her from getting stung by what I had heard was the largest beehive ever! Well, there's no arguing with my mom once she has her mind made up, especially when she wants to help me.

As we drove to the house, I took a deep breath. I had no idea what I was going to see or, even more importantly, what I was going to do. As I parked in the driveway, I asked my mom to wait on the back porch. After much convincing, she agreed.

My neighbor met me in the backyard. I could see lots of red welts all over both of his arms. He said the bee guy said to stay away from the back half of the property because the bees were angry, and they will attack anyone who makes any kind of movement. I listened to what he said, but I knew I had to go back there. I had to see my babies.

I asked God again for help, and I continued to walk. I had no plan. I had never been around swarms of bees. I really did not know what I was going to do. As I looked toward the barn, I saw the animals, and they had gone into the adjacent fenced acreage. They were still crying and screaming, and the horses were running sporadically all over while the little goats were crying and becoming stiff. They weren't able to walk very well, and some had uncontrolled movements with their limbs. I had to get there. The barn was still swarming wildly. Remembering that there was another entrance, I quickly headed for the street. We had built a gate in the front with a combination lock to allow for trucks to drive in. I hadn't gone through that gate in several years. I grasped the lock.

What was the combination? I thought.

I could still hear the crying and screaming of the animals. It was a sound I had truly never heard from any animal. I tried to move the combination lock and noticed that it was stuck. Drops of sweat fell right into my eyes as I strained to look at the tiny numbers. I finally got the numbers to move.

"Please, God, give me the combination. Please!"

I thought of a set of numbers, and it worked! After quickly opening the gate, I began to walk toward the back of the property where all the babies were. I saw Annabelle first, my sweet little goat, lying on her side, crying. I knew I had to go in and save them all, but I had no idea how to get them out especially in the condition that they were in. How was I to get them out, and where was I to put them? I felt prompted to pick up Annabelle. As I held her, I could see the others begin to walk toward me. I knew at that moment to walk back out of the gate and that they would all follow me. As I began walking, they all did follow me. All but one. Sophie, one of the little goats, was so disoriented. She ran in the wrong direction. She ran straight for the barn! I had Annabelle and all the others ready to go to safety. I continued to walk toward and on out of the gate. I kept walking all the way around and back into the property by the front where I had left my mom. On we went.

Annabelle continued to cry in my arms, but I could feel her breathing become less frantic. As I turned to look behind me, I could see all the animals walking behind me. I could see their pain, but I knew they trusted me to get them to safety. As I got close to the house, I carried Annabelle to the back deck where Mom was sitting, and I asked her to watch her.

As I laid her down, all I could see was what seemed like hundreds of welts all over her little body. Her legs and neck were stiff, probably from the venom of the beestings. My mom began to gently love on her. I remembered Sophie. I told my mom that I had to go back for one more. As I headed back into the fenced acreage, I remembered that she had run in the opposite direction. That meant toward the barn, where most of the bees were!

As I got to the halfway mark of the acre, I could see bees flying around. The barn was at the end of the acre. Sophie was nowhere in sight. At that moment, I just knew that she was inside the barn. I just knew it. The bee guy was right. There were so many bees around the barn. It looked like a huge dark cloud all around it. I was going to have to walk through all of that to get Sophie. I was afraid. I prayed again.

I could hear deep in my heart, "I will help you and protect you. Just keep walking."

I began to feel a calmness and I kept walking. I remembered what my neighbor had said about the bees and how they attack anyone who moves. I knew I had to save Sophie. She was scared and all alone in that barn full of angry bees. I couldn't just leave her there. I continued to walk slowly toward the barn. When I got to the door, I looked in and didn't see her.

I walked all the way in, and there, I saw her hiding way down underneath the milking stand, lying on her side. I called her name and told her that I loved her and that I would save her and get her out of there. She, too, was covered with welts all over, and her little legs and body were stiff. Her head was on the ground. I could see her breathing. Bees were everywhere. The air was so thick with them. I got this far. I was not going to stop. Not for anything. I had to squat down and lean far in and then grab her and gently pull her out. I didn't know where to grab her because I could tell she was in extreme pain. Finally, I found two places to hold, and I pulled her toward me. I gently lifted her and brought her close to my chest. As I stood up, I realized that I still needed to walk out of this bee infestation.

"Oh, God, please help me get out of here."

I could hear in my heart, "Trust Me. Just as you love Sophie and reached down to save her from this chaos and storm...I love you and I will reach down and save you from all of your chaos and storms in life. You are taking care of her the same way that I will take care of you. All you need to do is trust Me. Keep walking out."

I began to walk toward the gate, saying quietly under my breath, "The Lord is my shepherd... The Lord is my shepherd."

It felt as if I had been walking for miles, I was drenched in sweat. It seemed that there was not even one dry spot on my body. Large drops of sweat were rolling from my hair down my face and especially into my eyes. Halfway there, my arms began to shake from weakness, and I didn't think I could carry her anymore.

I said, "Your strength, not mine, Lord."

Immediately, Sophie felt light, and I had no problem carrying her out. As I came around to the house, I could see that my late husband and son were with my mom. Both of them were just standing there with their mouths open. I had just enough energy left to place Sophie on the deck next to Annabelle and fall over onto the deck in exhaustion. I glanced out into the pasture, and I could see that the horses and other goats were walking around and grazing on the grass. I was so thankful that they were okay.

As I laid there trying to catch my breath, I realized something amazing! I had just walked through what must have been thousands of swarming bees, and I had not been stung, not even one time! Not even one! I closed my eyes and thanked God in my heart.

I quickly opened my eyes to the crying and screaming from Annabelle and Sophie. They were still suffering. In the midst of all of this, it had become nighttime. I sent my mom home, and my late husband started dinner. I knew I had to do something for these babies tonight, so I set up my blankets and pillows in the old dog kennel. I didn't know where else to go with them. I gently carried each little goat over and placed them on soft blankets. I found a spot between them and sat down. I noticed that the roof was broken, and I had no covering.

Hopefully it doesn't rain tonight, I thought.

As I pulled them toward me, they continued to cry. Their breathing was still labored. They had welts everywhere. There were so many of them, even on their head and next to their eyes. I knew they were still in bad shape. I wanted to love on them, but where could I even place my hands so not to cause more pain? I placed my hands on their cheeks. Sophie's head was lying on my left thigh, and Annabelle's head was resting on my right thigh. I could only slightly move my fingers back and forth so as to not touch any of the welts. I began to sing softly to them. The first song that came to my mind was "Home on the Range." I tend to sing this tune when any of my little animals need me. As I sang, I prayed deep down in my heart, "Please, God, save them and heal them. I love them so!"

As I continued to sing and pray, I noticed that their breathing started to relax a little, and the crying began to slow down. As I leaned back against the pillow, I tried to stay awake and to keep singing. The sky was so clear, and there were so many stars. I noticed that they began to fall asleep. When I stopped singing, they would wake up. I kept singing and drifting off to sleep myself.

I eventually awakened to the beginning of a sunrise. I had been outside with them all night. Annabelle and Sophie were sleeping soundly on my lap with no crying or difficulty breathing. Suddenly, they both woke up and then stood up! No signs of stiffness or pain! They began to walk out toward the grass and joined the other animals grazing. As I sat there leaning back against the pillow, feeling physically exhausted, I knew in my heart that I was right in the center of many, many miracles. God had answered my prayers. My body was tired, but my heart was overflowing.

What had happened was much bigger than the amazing healing and restoration of the little animals. God had found me in my deepest despair. He heard me, and what's most important is I had heard Him too. I had heard Him in the middle of the swarm of bees, in my storm. I continued to sit there and think about how His message was clear, "Trust me. I love you and I will care for you." I had heard these messages before. I knew these words were in the Bible somewhere. The Bible is full of amazing inspirational quotes, but I really didn't know many of them. What I did know was that God had been talking to me. I knew it; with all of my heart, I knew it. I had believed in God pretty much all of my life, but I did not know that He would actually talk to me.

I was prompted to find these words in the Bible so that I wouldn't forget them. I had no idea where to look. Again, I asked God for help. I turned right to 1 Peter 5:7: "Cast all your care on Him because He cares for you." And Proverbs 3:5–6: "Trust in the Lord with all your heart and lean not on your own understanding;

in all your ways, acknowledge Him and He will make your paths straight."

Before, I used to think that the scriptures were important but just guidance or inspirational words. I had no idea that God was trying to talk to us. The miracle with the bees for me was beyond the physical healing. It was an awakening that God is really real, and He is trying to talk to me and to all of us. I wanted to hear Him again.

Finding Copper

I have a beautiful, copper-red, fluffy-eared cocker spaniel named Copper. He is truly darling. What makes him so precious is his love. He loves in a big way! He is bouncy like Tigger and does not hold back when he shows me how much he loves me. He gives big, wet, slobbery kisses and hugs with his two front paws wrapped around my neck and his head buried under my chin. He follows me everywhere. He truly exemplifies unconditional love. I know his favorite thing in the world is to be with me. He would choose to be with me over everything else, including food! After I feed him, he goes with me to feed the other animals. If I walk away before he finishes eating, he chooses to follow me than to finish his food. He would rather starve than to be away from me.

One day, when I had to go to work, we were having a very bad storm with thunder and lightning. I told him goodbye, kissed him on his velvety soft forehead, and reassured him that I would come back home. I asked my husband to watch him, so he would not try to follow me. I guess the storm had Copper very nervous, and he found a way to sneak out of the property in search of me. No one realized that he was gone until I got home from work because he usually stayed outside and would run and chase mynah birds all day. When I got home, I called for him. I called and called, and he didn't come. I had a terrible feeling in the pit of my stomach.

I knew something was terribly wrong. My little Copper boy was gone. I couldn't bear it. Everyone began to search and call for him. Some called the humane society and others called the radio stations. My heart hurt so bad I could barely stand it. Uncontrollable tears ran down my face.

I begged God to find him. "Please! Bring him home!"

I went outside to be alone. I found myself walking to be with all of my other animals on the farm, including my miniature goats, my big goats, sheep, potbellied pigs, chickens, cats, and a miniature rabbit. Each and every one of these have a special place in my heart, and they each have their own story of how they came to live on this farm. It's funny how often I get a new animal and, every time, it is some sort of a rescue situation.

As I walked to the back of the farm, I tried to somehow control my tears of sadness from missing Copper. I reached into Peter the rabbit's cage and gently picked him up, and he crawled up underneath my neck. I never get tired of the feel of his soft white fur and his gentle little nose wiggling against my skin. He licked me with his tiny red tongue. Who knew rabbits liked to lick you? I thought only dogs did. I sat down inside the barn and began to talk to them. I loved sitting with them and talking to them. I felt their love, and they somehow knew what I was saying or at least knew what I was feeling.

As I began to talk, I noticed that each one began to come closer. Before I knew it, they were all around me. Donald the goat is large and beige in color with one long horn and one short horn. He was "knock-kneed" and waddled back and forth when he walked. He came right up behind me and placed his cheek next to mine and his chin rested on my right shoulder. He remained very still in that position, and I could feel him breathing slow and steady. His fur was soft, and his breath was warm and sweet. It smelled of fresh clean hay. Daisy the goat came up next to me on my left. She put her head down next to my hand. I gently rubbed her cheek, and she closed her eyes. Ester my little handicapped potbellied pig came straight toward me. Her walk is unmistakable. You see, she was born with her hind legs deformed and had to practice very hard just to be able to walk. The thing about her that is so amazing is she doesn't think she is handicapped, and she never gives up. She practiced and practiced walking until she did it. She made her way to me, nuzzled her head into my lap, and pushed her wet rubbery snout against my legs. This is her way of giving kisses. Ruth the chicken came up next and sat down in the dirt nearby with her recently hatched babies following her. For a moment, I was distracted by watching how all her babies made their way underneath her. How did she fit ten babies under there? She was a wonderful mother and would die to protect them.

Lily and Mogley, our two female cats, walked up slowly and found their spots up on the rafters in the barn.

I loved them all, and they knew it. Somehow, they could feel my sorrow. How could they have known that I needed this? Before I even realized it, they had found a way to form a circle around me. A circle of love. I had tried to stop the tears, but I was unable to do so until now. Their love helped me calm down. I began to talk to them and explain what had happened to Copper. Somehow, I could sense that they knew what I was saying. Or at least they knew something had happened. Once again, I asked God to help me find Copper.

I woke up as the sun was rising. I had fallen asleep in the barn and been out there all night! Somehow, Peanut, my big, fluffy, brown sheep, had found a way to make himself a pillow for me. I could feel strands of wool falling off the side of my face as I sat up and tried to blink the blurriness away from my swollen eyes that I am sure came from crying so much. As I walked back to the house, once again, I begged God to find Copper. I moved through the day like molasses. We had no phone calls or leads to find Copper. None.

I got in the car and decided to drive up and down all the roads that I could and called and yelled for him. I drove around for what seemed like hours. My heart was heavy. I began to talk to God, and I started thanking God for giving me Copper and thanked Him for all the time that I had been given. I told God that Copper belonged to Him and that I knew that He was in charge. I knew that I should give Copper to God in my heart. He had always belonged to God. He was given to me to love and to care for. I told God I loved Copper and that I was sorry that he had gotten lost, and if He would give me another chance, I would do a better job. I also told God that if he didn't come home, I would just be thankful for the time I had been given. I asked God to take care of him no matter what happened.

The tears finally stopped, and for the first time since he had been missing, I felt peace. Right at that very moment, the phone rang, and it was my brother Mark.

"I found Copper!" he said.

I was speechless. *How could that be?* I thought. I had just given him back to God, just that very moment.

As I found my voice, I said, "What? How? Where is he?"

My brother came driving up just at that moment. "Jump in! Let's go get him!"

As we headed down the road, he explained that a lady had found him and put him in a kennel at her house, hoping that she could find his owner. As we drove up, I could see him curled up in the corner of the kennel. He looked so scared. My heart was pounding so fast with so many emotions. I couldn't help but run to him. As I got closer, he saw me. I opened the kennel door and called his name. He threw himself on me with such joy and love that it knocked me over, and he hugged me with his two front paws wrapped around my neck. He tucked his head under my chin. We were together again. I couldn't contain my tears. I told the lady thank you over and over and over. My brother and I got back into his truck with Copper by my side.

As we headed home, I thanked my brother so much for helping me. I explained that I had just been having a conversation with God and that I had given Copper back to Him and thanked God for the time I had been given.

Mark said, "That's what you needed to do so that God could teach you that we have to give everything to God."

I learned so much that day about love and about "letting go and letting God."

Charlotte and Sweet Pea

· · · · · · ·

One afternoon, I was just having a "normal day" on the farm. I was standing at the sink, washing dishes, and all of a sudden, I had an overpowering feeling to look outside in the front yard. I recognized this feeling. I had begun to learn that usually these "feelings" meant something. I had to find out what.

I raced to the front door. I looked in both directions. I noticed something that looked like a blur that appeared to be walking far down my road. At first, I didn't think it was important, but I had a strong prompting to pay attention and look closer. This "prompting" feeling became stronger. At that point, I knew something was wrong. I raced to find my rubber boots and ran down the stairs toward my front gate. As I got there, I noticed that the door to my two precious pet pigs' was slightly open! I looked inside and I saw it was empty! I knew that the "blur" that was headed down the road was my two potbellied pigs, Charlotte and Sweet Pea. I could feel my heart drop deep inside my chest. There are a lot of people who don't love pigs the way I do and only see them as a "meal."

I started running down our dirt road. We live in a very rural and agricultural area with dirt and gravel roads and large acre properties. The road felt like it went on forever. There was no sign of them anywhere. I was so scared for them. I was so focused on finding them that I hadn't even noticed that I was still in my pajama pants and that my two big goats, Daisy and Donald, were actually running behind me.

As I got toward the end of the road, I saw a truck pulled over toward the side and two men who looked like they were trying to catch something.

Oh my gosh! I thought. I knew at that moment that they were trying to capture Charlotte and Sweet Pea.

I had to act fast! I knew that if those men actually captured my girls that they would surely end up in their freezer.

I tried to run faster, and I began to yell. "Stop! Please! Those are my pigs!"

They both looked up toward me. I didn't recognize them. I knew that they were not my neighbors and didn't live close to me. I knew all of my neighbors.

I said it again, "Those are my pigs!"

One of the men seemed annoyed and said, "Why should I believe you? You have to prove that they are yours and I know you can't. They are just dumb old pigs. They won't listen to you anyway!"

Oh yeah? I thought.

I called them by name, and they came running to me. I petted each one on their heads and behind their ears. I could tell they were happy to see me. The two men glared at me. I looked in their hands and they were carrying ropes, chains, and a big cane knife. They also had a wire pig cage in the back of their truck.

The other man said, "I don't believe they are your pigs. We found them on the road, so they are ours now. Just turn around and go back home now. We are taking these two pigs, and you can't do anything about it."

My heart started pounding harder than it already was. I was too worried about my girls to be afraid. Right then, Daisy and Donald, my two big goats who by the way have very big and long and pointed horns, walked up right behind me. One stood on each side of me. The men noticed them right away.

One of the men laughed and said, "Ha! You think your goats can save your pigs?"

It's as if Donald and Daisy could hear and understand him! They immediately charged headfirst toward both men! These goats are strong and powerful when they want to be! Of course, they never were toward me.

All I could see was both men running and screaming, "No! Stop, stop, stop your goats! Take your stupid pigs already!"

I called Daisy and Donald by name, and they stopped. I looked at Charlotte and Sweet Pea, and they looked at me.

I gestured with my hand toward home and I said, "Let's go."

I turned toward home and, immediately, my pigs and goats came right beside me, and we all headed toward home. I didn't even look back at those men. I didn't want to. I just wanted to get home as fast as I could. As I began walking toward home, I glanced down at Charlotte and Sweet Pea. They were walking with me, instep with me without hesitation. I knew deep down that they were so happy that I had come for them and that they were ready to go home too. Daisy and Donald were a few steps behind us but following close behind as if they were still guarding us. As we walked toward home, my heart began to slow down to a somewhat normal beat.

It's then that I realized what had really happened. Daisy and Donald had followed me.

Why? I wondered. *What had prompted them to follow me? And how did they know to protect me and Charlotte and Sweet Pea from those two men?*

It had been amazing to watch. As I continued to walk, I remembered how it had all started. It started with a strong *prompting* or *gut feeling*. Whatever it's called, I could have easily missed it. What if I hadn't listened? What if I hadn't looked outside? I would have missed this chance to save Charlotte and Sweet Pea. They would probably be gone forever. I had an overwhelming thankfulness in my heart.

I reached out and patted both Daisy and Donald on their heads. As I did, they rubbed up against me and my pajama pants. They rubbed so hard that they actually pulled my pajama pants down! As I quickly grabbed my pants to pull them up, I noticed that no one was around at all. We were all alone on this dirt and gravel road, just the five of us. I began to laugh so loud and hard as I secured my pajama pants! I was so proud of my goats. They had been my heroes that day! I knew that we had really not been alone. The *prompting* or *gut feeling* had truly saved the day. I wanted to understand and to learn more about it. I said thank you deep within my heart. I knew something supernatural had happened that day.

A Conversation with My Horse

O n one very warm Sunday afternoon, I went outside for a walk to go check on my horse, Luke. I always loved my time with him. He was so beautiful. His color was light brown with a blond mane and a blond tail. As I walked toward him, he stopped grazing and put his head against my stomach, then he put his cheek against mine. I felt as if he was trying to tell me something, but I had no idea what it was. I loved his soft nose. His warm breath had a unique smell mixed with sweet hay.

This particular day was nice and warm with a soft breeze. I decided to take a little nap in my reclining beach chair underneath one of my coconut trees. As I laid there, I could see Luke far away on the other side of the property gently grazing. He was so beautiful to look at. As I stared at him, I remembered how I had heard that horses had a sort of sixth sense and could almost read our minds and communicate with us. I wondered if it was true.

Then all of a sudden, I had a crazy "thought" or "prompting." I should try an experiment to see if horses really can read our minds and communicate. After thinking for a little while, I had a plan. I decided that I would "ask" Luke to do something just with my mind, using only my thoughts. I wanted to ask him something specific so that it couldn't be mistaken for a coincidence. I relaxed and closed my eyes and began to ask Luke to come to me and to place his nose onto my right hand.

I repeated this phrase, "Luke, walk to me please and put your nose on the top of my right hand." I repeated this phrase over and over in my head while visualizing him actually doing it. I kept my eyes closed the whole time.

All of a sudden, I felt something very soft and warm on the top of my right hand! I opened my eyes quickly, and I couldn't believe what I saw! Luke was standing next to me with his nose on the top of my right hand! I truly couldn't believe it!

As amazing as this seemed, I couldn't help but think it was just a coincidence or that Luke had just by chance walked over to me and had wanted to touch my hand just to be affectionate. I decided that I had to do it again. This time, I waited for him to go back to grazing and then I did the exact same thing except I asked him to walk over to my left side and place his nose on the top of my left hand. I could not believe it! Within five minutes, he actually touched the top of my left hand with his nose!

This time, I was convinced that it was not a coincidence. It was too specific. I knew that something amazing had happened, but how? Luke had heard me somehow and followed my request. Then I remembered that earlier, I had a feeling that maybe Luke was trying to tell me something. Was he? I had a *thought* or *prompting* to test it. What if I had ignored this? I would have missed this amazing miraculous blessing. I had a lot to think about. I was so very thankful; and my heart was so full of love for Luke, and I could feel his love for me. I wanted to know more.

Lil' Henry

Have you ever had a "feeling" that you needed to do something that you either ignored or hoped would just go away? Well, this happened to me on this one particular beautiful, late, sunny afternoon.

I had a good reason to ignore it, or so I told myself when I had that first feeling to go check on my little goats way back on the property in the barn. I had just brought my mom over to my house to look at my vegetable aquaponics garden, so she could pick some eggplants and green tomatoes, which was her favorite thing to fry up. Coming from the South, this was practically a delicacy. Her coming over was a big thing because we were in the middle of a COVID-19 pandemic. My mom had been isolating, and I have been her only contact, mainly taking her out for drives and shopping for her groceries (I made her stay in the car). She hadn't been outside in months and months, except to walk to the car from her house.

As she sat in my "open" greenhouse, it was very pleasant with a nice breeze that seemed to cool us off from the afternoon heat just perfectly. She had needed my help up the stairs for support. Being isolated from COVID-19 had changed her level of activity, and I could see she had lost some strength and endurance. But after she got up the steps, she had no trouble walking all around excitedly as I showed her my huge tomato plants; beautiful, shiny, bright purple eggplants; cucumbers that had just begun to bloom into "tiny, little pickles," as I called them; okra; tiny, little bell peppers that had grown on tiny bell pepper plants; and a wide variety of lettuces.

As we walked around, I kept thinking, *I need to go check on the goats.* Then I would tell myself that I would go as soon as I took my mom back home. I even told my mom that I needed to go make sure they were okay and make sure they had water.

My mom quickly said, "No problem, I can go ahead and go home."

As I once again helped my mom down the steps and head back to the car, I thought to myself, *It will be okay to wait and check on the goats when I get back home.*

As I pulled back into my driveway, I turned on the long water hose and put it first into the big goat water barrel and then I headed back to the barn. As I entered the gate, I began to count the goats as I did every day. They often would come to greet me as soon as I came in. As I began to count, I gazed past the first group of four little Nigerian dwarf goats, and I saw one down. My heart felt like it had stopped. Anytime there was a goat down, it was a very bad sign. I knew it all too well. Having been raising these little guys for at least six to seven years, I had my fair share of "goats down." They are so fragile. I had started with two females and quickly grew to sixteen. During this time, I had lost some precious little ones. I attempted to help each one by either resuscitation, spoon-feeding, holding them in my arms for many an "all nighter," massaging their little bloated tummies, but each time, they had not pulled through.

When I saw a "goat down," I recognized him right away as my newest little fellow. He was very special. They all are, but he "came to me" one week after my husband had died from a yearlong of suffering with a terrible stage-four stomach cancer. A lady had called me "out of the blue" to ask if I would take her little goat and care for him because she could no longer do it. He and his brother had been gifts for her kids, and after her little goat's brother died, this little fellow cried day and night. At first, I was hesitant because I was in my own world of grief, but I thought, *What's one more goat?* As soon as I said yes, she came over.

I knew he was a Nigerian dwarf which is a miniature goat, but I didn't expect him to be so tiny. He was the smallest Nigerian dwarf goat I had ever seen, and he was full grown. As soon as she lifted him out of her car and placed him on the ground, he walked right up to me. I reached down and picked him up in my arms, and he pressed himself next to me.

The lady waved as she drove away and yelled, "Oh, by the way, his name is Lucifer! You can change his name if you want to."

What! I would never name any of my animals that.

I looked at him, and he tucked his head under my chin and nuzzled in my neck.

"I will give you a new name," I told him.

I headed for the barn. Knowing goats, I knew there was an introductory period. He had to be accepted. Unbeknownst to most people, goats have many feelings and emotions. Jealousy is one of them. As soon as I introduced him, I could sense jealousy among them. I put him down to walk. The others at first ignored him. I noticed that he was different from the others. He walked very slowly, and he had a fat belly. I remember thinking that they must have just fed him before they brought him over. Looking back now, if I had not been dealing with such grief with losing my husband, I would have asked a lot more questions. I had at least asked if he had been wormed. She said that he and his brother had previously had a bad case of worms, but she gave the worming medicine, and he was all clear.

I thought I would leave him for a while in with the others and watch from afar. As soon as I walked away, he began to cry. I went back inside and held him in my lap, and he quietly calmed down. Again, he tucked his head in my neck. The other goats didn't want anything to do with him. I had to go pick up supplies at the feed store. I decided to take him with me. I had some diapers in the house from other little goats (I have had many an adventure with little goats). I knew how to put a diaper on a goat and make it fit so no leaks. So that is what I did.

Off we went. The little goat, my cocker spaniel, Copper, and me. Copper took his usual place on the console between the two front seats. He would rest his two front paws on it and stand on his two hind legs in the back seat. He knew he was my copilot. The little goat sat himself down on the floor of the passenger seat and just looked up at me. This was the first time that I had actually looked him in the eyes. What beautiful gentle eyes he had. In that moment, I knew it was meant to be. I was supposed to have him, and he was supposed to have me. He stayed in that position the whole time I drove around to do my errands. I had to get out of my truck for just a moment to order and pay for some gravel. As soon as I stepped out, he got up in the seat and started crying as loud as he could. When I got back inside, I patted him on the head and told him not to worry and that I wouldn't leave him and that he was safe with me. He got back onto the floor of the truck and sat down and once again looked up at me.

I thought to myself, *This little goat isn't like any of my other goats. There is something special about him.*

As the days went on, I spent a lot of time with him back in the barn helping him feel accepted by the others and loved by me. He needed a new name. I talked with my kids, and we decided that he looked like a "Henry," which happened to be my late husband's middle name. I thought it was very appropriate because of the timing of when I got him. I thought maybe he was a little gift from God to keep me distracted during my grief and attempts to heal. So we started calling him Lil' Henry.

He learned his name very quickly. Another unusual sign. It usually takes goats at least a little time to learn their names. I soon began to notice his belly was swelling up.

"Oh no!" I remember thinking, *This is never a good sign.*

I began to study to remind myself what to do. I gave him baking soda, inspected his droppings for signs of parasites, watched him eat and drink. The bloating finally went away, then he got diarrhea. This was a bad sign. I got help from a vet and ended up giving him three rounds of worming medicine and began a regime of B-12 because he was anemic.

Over the course of seven months, he slowly began to actually get better. He had always walked slowly from the moment I had gotten him, but now he was finally walking with a spring in his step. He would actually walk fast to follow me around. I would sit every day in the barn with the goats all around me and Lil' Henry in my lap. This brought me so much peace and healing and happiness. The goats began to accept him, especially one of my very old goats named Francis. Francis was actually one of my rescue "full-size" goats that I had won at a feed store raffle drawing. He is a "meat" goat. I had entered a drawing one day just to get the advertised discount.

I had no intention of winning that goat. I remember some cowboys who stood behind me distinctly saying, "I hope I win that goat, so I can put him on my grill for a delicious dinner."

I wasn't going to stay for the drawing, but my late husband insisted. "Let's see if we win," he said.

Sure enough, they actually called my name! We didn't even have a crate or anything to carry him home in. Those cowboys overheard us talking about not having any way to get him home, and they offered to take him "off our hands." I knew their intentions and I knew I had to save him.

"No, thank you," I said. "We will manage."

We put him in the back seat of our minivan and headed home. Needless to say, he left us a lot of little pellet surprises. He has been part of the family ever since. Francis had taken Lil' Henry under his wing, so to speak. It was so sweet to watch.

As I saw the "goat down," I quickly recognized that it was Lil' Henry. I raced over to his little apparently lifeless body and grabbed him up, bringing him close to my chest in the position he loved to be carried in. In that instant, my world felt like it was crashing in again. I kept pacing back and forth, hugging him so tightly.

"No, no, no!" I yelled and sobbed all at the same time. "No!"

The tears came falling out. I had learned with the very recent passing of my late husband that there is a big difference from crying for a sad movie or a sad story, and then there is crying from a place inside of you that you didn't even know existed. If these tears and crying could be described in a tangible way, it would be like a rockslide avalanche, or a volcano that erupts from a deep place that you had never even discovered that began to come up and out with such uncontrollable force with the pain being in your head and your heart. Not really physical pain but true anguish like a fire that you cannot put out.

At that moment of holding Lil' Henry, I was quickly transported right back to the same feelings of despair and loss that I had had with the very recent loss of my late husband. I found myself sitting and holding Lil' Henry so tightly, putting his head under my neck, and rocking him back and forth, saying the same things that I had said when I was watching my late husband slowly disappear and die from the cancer that had ravaged his body.

You see, he had gotten a diagnosis of stomach cancer and went through three rounds of chemotherapy. He had gotten the "all clear" from a PET scan and was told he was cancer-free for the third time in his life! He had beaten cancer! He even rang the bell at the Cancer Center. But just two months later, it came back with a vengeance. I had taken off a lot from work and gave all of my attention and effort with everything I had to help care for him and help heal him.

When it came back, I remember thinking, *Well, I will do it again. I will do everything I can to keep this man alive!*

That's what I did. I gave it my all and then some. I lost twenty pounds, and the fatigue and constant neck pain and muscle strain was almost unbearable. But I knew what he was feeling was so much worse that I didn't give any thought to my pain. There were days in the hospital that I didn't even eat. Sometimes because I couldn't because of no appetite, and other times because we didn't have any money. Without me working, we had become so poor. My late husband would tell me to eat part of his food on his tray. He knew I wasn't eating. I would only eat if I knew he was done. I only did it because I knew I had to eat, so I could continue to care for him. When he got too sick to eat, they stopped ordering him a food tray. I then had to stop eating too. I was okay with it. My only focus was keeping him alive.

I checked his skin. I repositioned him. I did range of motion to his arms and legs. I massaged his feet and shoulders. I covered him and uncovered him, which he needed about every twenty minutes around the clock. The fatigue was like being slowly choked at your neck. I cried only when he was asleep, or when I was in the shower. I refused to believe he was dying.

After he died, I felt guilty that I had not done enough to keep him alive. I would cry and say, "I'm sorry if I missed something, if I didn't do something that would have kept you alive longer." I went into a type of denial or avoidance place. The covid-19 situation was perfect for me. I had a great excuse to not have a funeral. I didn't want to have one. I wasn't ready. I couldn't look at any photos or videos of him. It was too painful. I began to grow vegetables, and I spent time with my goats to get distracted.

As I held Lil' Henry in my arms, I cried and sobbed, and I heard myself say out loud all the same thoughts that I had recently had about my late husband. My two adult daughters came outside to check on me.

I just kept sobbing and hugging and rocking him in my arms, saying, "I'm sorry, I'm sorry, I'm so sorry."

I knew I had a feeling that I needed to come check on the goats. I should have come out sooner. I tried so hard to take of care of him and heal him and keep him alive. I loved him and he loved me. He was my partner; he would sit with me, and we spent time together. I tried to keep him alive! I tried to heal him! I cried and sobbed and repeated those words over and over and over.

It became dark and the night was getting late. My girls showed their strength that night. In the darkness, they got a shovel and a pick. My oldest of the two passed her infant to the other and began to dig. This was a feat in and of itself because we don't have dirt, only lava rock. It took her a long time to dig a hole big enough for Lil' Henry to fit in. We had all known the loss of many pets over the years, but my late husband was always the one to dig the holes and bury them. He did the "dirty work" because he loved us. We had to figure this one out without him.

My younger daughter asked if we could plant her newly bought lemon tree with him. I thought it was a great idea. I asked my girls if they could see the parallel or metaphor with losing Lil' Henry and their dad. They quickly nodded their heads yes. As I sat in the barn holding him, I had a "knowing" that this whole thing was a metaphor or parallel to my life. It was strong. It was like God was telling me at that moment all the similarities and that I was going through all of it as a way of "letting go" even down to having to bury him and "have a funeral." It was the physical act of going through this process. As I rubbed his soft fur, I was brought back in time to snapshot memories of the stages of my late husband's illness and his dying process. This had been the worst thing I had ever experienced in my life, and the anguish was unbearable to think about. That's why I had gone into denial or avoidance.

So when I bonded with Lil' Henry then had to "let him go," all my emotion from losing my late husband came flooding out. I cried that night until I couldn't cry any more. My nose was completely plugged, and I had a pounding headache. But I did finally stop crying, and I had talked my way from "I'm sorry, I could and should have done more to save you" to "I did everything I could to save you and God has you now." I knew I couldn't have changed anything if I had come out a little earlier.

My girls offered to place him into the grave for me, but I knew I had to do it. I knew God wanted me to do it as part of my healing process to learn to begin to "let go." My girls and I sat on the grass next to the hole under a full moon. We talked about God, and they shared with me that our understanding of God is like taking a cup and scooping up water in a big ocean. We can keep scooping up water to keep learning, but we will never understand the vastness of God. They reminded me how much He loves us and how we need to hold on to that. They also said my late husband is at peace and is in the arms of the Comforter.

As I lifted Lil' Henry's body and placed him into the grave, I finally felt a little peace, and I told him that I loved him and thanked him for loving me. We placed the lemon tree inside with him and covered them. I said the prayer (I knew it had to be me as part of this journey or season of learning to let go).

I have been thinking lately that if we don't get the lesson, life will give us the lesson. I learned so much that day, and I thanked God.

Ester

H ave you ever felt pulled in two different directions, and you were desperately needed in both places? Well, this happened to me.

I had a very pregnant pig, and I was also very needed at my full-time job because most of our staff had called out sick due to a flu outbreak. I was prompted to go out and check on Charlotte, my pregnant pig, before I left for work. I remember looking at Charlotte and Charlotte looking back at me, and for a moment, I thought I could feel Charlotte telling me "It's time." I had to go to work. I had no choice. The family depended on my paycheck to survive. I had been feeling pulled between being at work and being at home for many years now. My heart had been calling me to be home, home with my children, my animals, and my late husband who had recently been through a very serious bout of nasopharyngeal cancer requiring extensive chemotherapy and radiation treatments. I was grateful for my job. I had worked hard to earn my degree as an occupational therapist, and I knew that helping people had been my calling. But my priority was my family and my amazing animals. I seemed to know when my animals needed me. I could sense when they were sick or in trouble. I thought this was normal and that everyone could feel these things, but when I talked about this, most people just looked at me with blank stares.

After I checked on Charlotte, I had to stop thinking about her or the guilt would just eat away at me. My focus quickly changed to getting to work on time, and I forgot about that "connection." After I got to work, I was prompted to text my daughter frequently throughout the day, asking for details about Charlotte like how Charlotte was acting, what position she was in, how was she breathing, etc. My daughter was very willing to go check on her each time because she understood how guilty I felt leaving Charlotte when I knew she needed me the most.

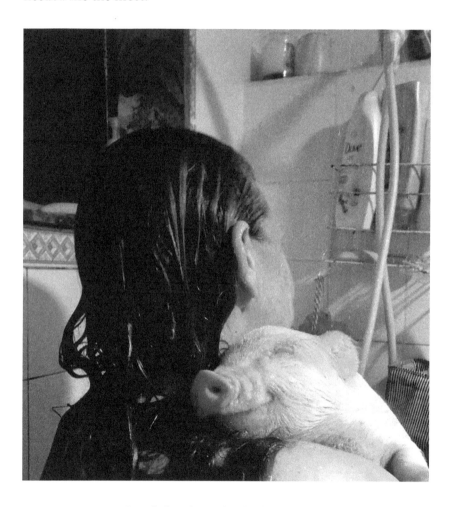

During my lunch break, I checked my phone messages again. *Oh no!* My daughter texted that when she last checked on her, there were a whole lot of tiny, little piglets all around Charlotte! I couldn't believe it! Charlotte was trying to tell me that she was going to give birth today, and I didn't listen. I wanted to go home so badly but I couldn't, but I felt a strong prompting to do so. I actually had an extra-busy day with more than normal paperwork. I tried to work as quickly as I could to finish everything.

When I finally finished my workday, I had to stop by the store to get milk and bread and prescription medication for my late husband. Then I had to fight unusually heavy traffic. It felt as if I would never get home. When I did finally make it home, I jumped out of my truck and ran to the back of the property to my barn where Charlotte had given birth. I had to go through several gates with lots of dogs, goats, and sheep who were all very happy to see me and rushed up for affection.

I finally reached Charlotte. She was lying down on her side, nursing eight little piglets. She looked so peaceful, and all the babies had latched on to her successfully and were getting their nourishment. I was so thankful for that. Out of the corner of my eye, I noticed that the ground began to move! Not like an earthquake or anything, but a small patch of dirt began to move very slightly. I couldn't help but stare at this. The movement began to slow down. It suddenly occurred to me that it could be another baby pig! I rushed down to pick it up. It was a tiny, little piglet! I noticed that it was a little girl. She was cold and very dirty, and her little mouth and eyes were open and filled with dirt. I could feel a faint heartbeat. This little piglet was so small that it fit in the palm of my right hand. This little pig was probably moments from death. I said a deep prayer in my heart for help.

As I raced back to the house, I pressed its little body under my neck, trying to give it body heat. I could feel her heartbeat against my neck, and I couldn't help but notice how incredibly cold this baby was.

I whispered in her ear, "Please don't die!"

When I finally got to the house, I placed her down on a soft towel. I frantically began to look for the hair dryer. I had to somehow warm her up. I searched everywhere. I ended up digging in all the drawers in the bathroom and in all the dresser drawers in all the bedrooms. It was nowhere!

Again, I said, "Help me, please."

Suddenly, I found it, and it was in the very last place that I had thought to look. By this time, my heart was beating out of my chest and sweat was pouring down my face and burning my eyes. I rushed to plug the hair dryer in as I tried to wipe the sweat away, but my hands began to shake as I tried to dry my hands to keep the moisture out of the plug. I knew I was quickly running out of time.

Why is it taking so long to just get this baby warmed up? I thought.

Finally, I was able to begin to apply heat to this little one. As she began to warm up, I looked at her little eyes that were fixed in an open position and were filled with dirt. Her mouth was also open a little and filled with dirt too. Her little body was so cold, but her heartbeat suddenly began to get a little stronger. I couldn't help but wonder if I was too late. I continued to ask for help deep in my heart. Within about ten to fifteen minutes, she began to move her hands and feet. Then her head began to move. Then all of a sudden, she began to blink her eyes! Then she tried to suck on her fingers!

Could she be coming back from the brink of death? I wondered.

Within half an hour, she actually attempted to walk, and she was warm and able to maintain her own body heat. It was truly a miracle. It was then that I actually was able to take a good look at her. Even though I had only been with her for a short time, I already loved her.

Now what? What should I do with her now? I thought.

I knew that if she were to survive, she would need to nurse from her mother. So I picked her up and headed back to the barn. I was worried that the mom wouldn't accept her because she had been handled by a human.

As I approached Charlotte, she was still nursing the other babies and didn't even seem to notice that anyone had come into the barn. I gently placed the little one down next to her, and she latched on with just a few short attempts. Charlotte opened her eyes and looked right at me. As we looked at each other, I felt that she was saying thank you. She wiggled a little and adjusted herself as if to make room for her new little precious baby. Then she sat up and nudged her with her snout, then she laid back down and closed her eyes.

Oh boy! What an adventure! I thought.

I had been trying so hard to save her life, I hadn't even noticed that she was handicapped. Her back legs had bony deformities so severe that it looked as if she would never walk. I didn't care. I made a promise that I would take care of her, and I would even build adapted wheels if she needed it, and I will make sure that she has a good life.

As I stood there just watching her, I decided that she needed a name. I wanted her to feel loved and accepted especially because of her deformities, and I specifically want her to know that she was beautiful and that she has a great purpose to be alive. I decided to name her Ester, after Ester in the Bible. She was a beautiful person on the inside and on the outside. She gave up everything to save her people.

I took a deep breath feeling confident that she was now doing well, and then I remembered how this day had started. It had begun with several promptings and a "connection" that I had felt from Charlotte. What if I had ignored that prompting? What if I hadn't noticed that little movement in the dirt? What if I hadn't tried to revive little Ester? I knew deep in my heart that I had witnessed a true miracle, and I knew that I could have so easily missed it if I had ignored any of those *promptings*. I was so thankful, and I had another prompting. The prompting was telling me that Ester had great purpose and that soon it would be revealed to me.

I remember thinking, *I hope I can continue to get better and better at hearing these promptings*. I wanted to learn more.

Sweet Pea the Pig

M y darling little pink potbellied pig has been one of my greatest joys. She really exemplifies her name. All I have to do is call her and she comes to me no matter where she is. She has total trust in me and knows that I love her, will take care of her, and will never bring harm to her. Pigs by nature are prey animals, so they are always wary of others and have the fight-or-flight responses. They are quick to respond to loud noises or new situations and, oftentimes, respond with defensive behavior.

She was recently pregnant with her second litter. I moved her out of the pen with the others and into a private pen with lots of soft straw in preparation for the big day. I have been checking on her many times during each day, thinking "today is the day." My late husband and son were recruited to do the same. It became such routine that they started to believe that maybe she was never going to give birth. I was beginning to wonder if she was getting way overdue.

One Saturday morning, I had to go in to work, which was unusual as I usually didn't work on Saturdays. I checked on her like I normally had been doing, and I noticed that she was lying on her side. I didn't think much of it, and I tossed her food in as usual. What I did notice was that she did not get up right away for her food. She finally did get up but a bit slower than normal. I just thought that she was moving slowly because she had gotten so big. I was really just focused on getting to work on time. However, I did have this "thought" or "prompting" deep inside of me that said, "Sweet Pea will give birth today." I mentioned it to my late husband and son that I thought today was the day for Sweet Pea to give birth and could they please check on her more often. He and my son were watching TV and they grunted "Okay" and continued to watch their show.

I left for work, which was providing occupational therapy treatment to patients in their own homes. When I had finished with the treatment sessions, I called home to tell my husband that I was done and wanted to go get groceries for the next week. As an afterthought, I asked him to get my son to check on Sweet Pea.

I could hear my son through the phone saying, "There's one baby pig in with Sweet Pea!"

"What!" I yelled.

All I could think of was that I knew she was going to give birth today, but I didn't pay attention to the *prompting*.

"I'm coming home now!" I said to my late husband. I asked him to please make sure she was all right until I could get there.

All the way home, I could feel excitement welling up inside of my heart. I just kept smiling and feeling thankful. I loved the times of birthing on my little farm. The idea of new life is awesome.

When I arrived, I quickly changed clothes and went to Sweet Pea. Sure enough, there it was. A tiny, little, pink baby potbellied pig. I could see that it was a little boy. Sweet Pea was lying on her side. I noticed that she was breathing a little heavy but nothing too concerning, or so I thought. I was anxiously awaiting the next baby to be born. After about an hour, I became very aware of the fact that nothing was happening. Nothing. I tried to reposition her, but she wanted to remain lying down on her side. After about two hours, she began to shake a little bit harder but still no babies were being born. I decided to research her symptoms and found out that if no other babies or the after birth did not come within thirty minutes of the first birth of a baby pig, then I should become concerned.

Oh boy! I thought.

The next instructions were quite specific. I must enter the pig to retrieve the babies or facilitate the passing of the after birth.

Oh my goodness! Was I even able to do this? I wondered.

I headed out to the barn to get all of my supplies. I knew I had to try. I had to try to save the babies, but even more importantly,

I had to save my precious Sweet Pea. First, I cut my fingernails. Then I gathered together my disposable rubber gloves and corn oil. I removed my jewelry and had my son look up the anatomy of a pig on his phone to provide some sort of guide for this procedure. I tried at least five different times, but each time, I was unable to complete this. She was very uncomfortable and would not let me. I knew very soon that the outcome was now out of my hands. I asked for help deep down inside my heart. I didn't want her to die. I became afraid for her life. I noticed that she was feeling warm from the summer heat, so I set up a fan to blow gently on her. I wanted to let her know that I loved her and was there for her.

I spread out an old blanket on the soft straw next to her in the pen, and I laid down next to her. She loved to be rubbed behind her ears and on her belly. I began to sing songs to her while I rubbed on her. I knew that she felt loved, and I also knew that she loved me. The connection was amazing. I rolled over and wrapped my arms around her as if to give her a big hug, placing my head next to hers. Again, I asked for help for Sweet Pea deep down in my heart. We fell asleep together.

I woke up suddenly and checked on her and checked on the time. We had slept for five hours! Too much time had gone by with no change. My mom came by on her way home from errands and checked on Sweet Pea's progress. She noticed that Sweet Pea was beginning to move around a little and thought that maybe she would begin to give birth again.

To our surprise, a baby came falling out! It was a healthy little baby girl! This was truly a miracle. From all that I had read and learned about pigs giving birth, it was unheard of to have such a large amount of time between deliveries of babies in mammals. Death was surely imminent with this much time lapse, or so they say.

Within thirty minutes, out popped another healthy baby girl! After thirty more minutes, out popped another baby! It was a healthy baby boy! Sweet Pea was lying on her side and began nursing all of her new babies. What an amazing site to see. I knew that I was witnessing a true miracle. I had asked for help from deep down inside my heart and help was given. I was so thankful. I knew that it was not over yet though. She had to pass the afterbirth to ensure her own safety and good health.

I continued to stay with her for four more hours, but nothing happened. Again, I asked for help deep in my heart. I felt a prompting that I could go inside the house and go to bed. It had gotten very late at night, and I was totally exhausted.

At four in the morning, I was prompted to go outside and check on her. Lo and behold, she had indeed passed the afterbirth! I knew that the *prompting* had actually awakened me from sleep so that I could witness this. I went back to bed very comforted that Sweet Pea would now be okay.

By morning, Sweet Pea and her four healthy little ones were walking all around the pen just as happy as ever. I had witnessed a great miracle.

For most folks, this would probably seem very trivial. For me, I knew beyond any doubt that my Sweet Pea and her babies had been saved. It had truly been supernatural. I'm beginning to realize how important those little *promptings* really are, and more importantly, how important it is to actually listen to them.

There's Always Hope

I found myself sitting outside in my barn with all of my little miniature goats. This is my favorite place to be, especially when I'm feeling sad.

Today was one of those days. I was really missing my brother. He had died recently from a sudden death from a very bad asthma attack. I couldn't believe that he was actually gone. He would never come walking up my driveway to visit me ever again. I was so sad that my heart hurt. When he was alive, I had given him one of my baby goats. It was a little girl goat, and he named her Olive. She was so sweet. I had to keep her at my farm for a while because he was working out of town. I still had Olive at my farm when he died. She became mine.

The day after my brother died, one of my momma goats gave birth to a tiny, little baby boy goat. He was so tiny and precious. I fell in love with him immediately. I wanted to name him after my brother, so I called him Little Mark. He grew up to be such a wonderful goat with such a sweet disposition. I was able to have a few babies from him, and they all turned out to be wonderful goats. And the best part was knowing that they were from my little goat who was named after my brother.

When Little Mark was born, he was extra small; in fact, he was the tiniest baby goat I had ever seen. Soon, I began putting him in diapers, and I took him everywhere. Little Mark was born during a season in my life in which my late husband and I would go downtown and feed the homeless every week and try to bring them some kind of message of hope. Soon, Little Mark came along with us.

From the first day, it became quite clear that Little Mark was supposed to be there with us.

On his first day with us, I noticed a man by the name of Joe. He was one of the folks that came to eat with us. He was in a wheelchair and always looked very, very sad. He had been talking to me about his life's journey and that his sister had been killed by a drunk driver, his brother had died of cancer, and how he himself had been in a very bad car accident that left him disabled and cost him his job, which has now caused him to be homeless on the streets. I felt prompted to ask him if he would mind holding Little Mark for a while, so I could unpack some things. He quickly agreed and reached out his hands. As I gave Little Mark to him, I noticed how Joe was so gentle and kind to him. He made sure that Little Mark was comfortable sitting on his lap. He began to pet him and rub his tiny, little head. Soon, Joe began sharing about how he grew up on a farm, which was a happy time in his life with his family. He told me stories of saving a baby calf, and how the calf would follow him everywhere. I could see tears in his eyes. He held Little Mark the whole time we were there.

When it was time to leave, he thanked me over and over for letting him hold Little Mark and begged me to bring him back again next week. Although he thanked me, it was I who felt great gratitude. As I listened to Joe tell his stories, I couldn't help but think of my brother Mark and how I missed him so very much and how it seemed so surreal to have his goat's baby with me. It almost felt like Mark was with me. I shared with Joe about the loss of my brother and that the goat he was holding was named after him. Joe looked at me with so much compassion as if he knew at that point that he was not alone with his suffering.

One day, when I went outside to check on my animals, I saw from far away that one of my goats was lying on the ground. I was so worried that I ran as fast as I could to see who it was. It was Little Mark. He was lying very still and barely breathing. I grabbed him up into my arms and held him so tightly. I put my cheek next to his, and I cried and cried. It almost felt like I was losing my little brother all over again. I decided that I would never name any of my animals after people that I love ever again. It's too painful when they pass away.

Little Mark passed away slowly in my arms. My late husband came back there and gently took him out of my arms and found a special place to bury him. I was not only sad about losing Little Mark, but I also realized that his legacy ended with him. I would never have another little goat from him ever. As a matter of fact, he was my last male goat, so I wouldn't have any more babies at all unless I found another male. For the next few weeks, I couldn't stop thinking about the death of my little brother and the death of my little goat, Little Mark. My heart was heavy.

I tried to carry on with life as best as I could. I continued to have sad days sometimes, but I tried to keep moving forward. One day, about four or five months later, as I was driving home from work, I had a very strong prompting to get home quickly and go check on my goats in the barn. As soon as I drove into the driveway, the *prompting* became even stronger. As I parked my truck, I felt compelled to get back to the barn as fast as I could. So I began to run toward the barn. As soon as I got there, I saw one of my little girl goats, Renée, all alone right outside the barn. I didn't pay much attention to her at first. Then I realized that she was standing unusually still. I decided to go up close to her to see if she was okay.

Right as I walked up to her, I couldn't believe what I saw! She began to give birth right before my eyes! I didn't even know that she was pregnant! I had nothing prepared! I didn't have a place in the barn ready or even any birthing supplies on hand. It happened so fast! I stood there in total awe. After the baby was born, I noticed that it was a tiny, little girl. I watched as Renée tried to clean her baby and then I watched the baby start to stand up and walk. At that point, I couldn't help but notice that the baby was so small that she could not even reach Renée's udders to begin nursing. I knew I had to intervene. I squatted down next to both of them and lifted her up and held her there, trying to help her latch on, so she could nurse from her mother. It didn't go very well. Renée didn't want to stand there and let her baby nurse. She began eating grass and drinking water. I decided to milk Renée to get some of her colostrum and put it in a bottle for the baby. It was vital that the baby get some nourishment soon. So I did just that. I brought the baby inside the house and began trying to give her the bottle. She actually began to drink, and she drank a lot of it! Then she cuddled up in my hand and fell asleep.

As I sat there holding this precious little, tiny one in the palm of my hand, I started to realize what had just happened. I had no idea that Renée was pregnant, and Little Mark had died at least four or five months ago. He was the only male that I had in my goat herd. Then I thought about this new little baby goat. She had to be a daughter from Little Mark! His lineage hadn't died off after all! I couldn't believe it! I had this new little baby girl goat. It's like she brought me a message of hope.

Hope! I will name her Hope! I thought.

As I sat there holding little baby Hope, I had so many thoughts swirling inside of my head. I was thinking of how I could have missed out on seeing baby Hope being born. If I hadn't followed the prompting to go outside and check on my goats, I would have not even known that Renée was pregnant. She was just standing outside when she gave birth. What if it had been raining? What if I hadn't found them and the baby wasn't able to get her first nourishment? She would have surely died. Then I thought of the fact that Renée must have gotten pregnant from Little Mark right before he died.

My little Renée, the one who had a stillborn baby a few years ago, had just given birth to a healthy baby girl, and my beloved little goat named after my brother had been able to leave a legacy months after he had gotten sick and died. God had seen Renée's pain and loss, and He had seen mine. He blessed us both. Sometimes, we can feel sad and lost from difficult situations and wonder if God even hears us. What I witnessed today was truly a gift from God, and He was saying to me and to Renée that He loves us. I had been so incredibly sad when he died and that he wasn't going to have an offspring to keep his memory continuing on. It really seemed like a miracle. I couldn't help but smile. My heart was so full. I felt happy. This was something that I had not felt in such a long time. It was as if a small piece of my little brother was somehow still with me.

Pollyanna

One very cold and rainy day, just around Thanksgiving, we had a tiny, little baby dwarf Nigerian goat born on our farm. She was so incredibly small. I realized that she was so small, she must be a premature baby. Her mother was not interested in trying to nurse her and kept leaving her outside in the rain. I knew I had to act quickly, so I took her into the house and started bottle-feeding her. At first, she had a very hard time learning to drink from the bottle. I kept trying over and over, and finally, she began to drink. She was so small that she fit in the palm of my hand. She was maybe five inches in length at the most. I was already in love with her. I put her next to my neck underneath my chin, and I could feel her little body rest against mine.

I could feel her tiny, little heartbeat. I remember thinking at that moment that nothing else mattered in the whole world except loving her and helping her. She was solid white with big beautiful brown eyes. Her fur was softer than cotton, and she smelled so incredibly sweet.

She needs a name, I thought.

All of a sudden, I remembered one of my favorite childhood movies called *Pollyanna*, which was about this special little girl that brought happiness to all the people in her little town.

Pollyanna it is! I thought.

Suddenly, I realized that if I was going to care for her, I had to really start thinking and planning. Thankfully, this was not my first baby goat born on my farm, so I had some supplies on hand. I had purchased milk replacement and even premature baby diapers (I had secretly always wanted to have a baby goat that I could put in diapers and take everywhere with me!). As I began to research this, I soon realized that I would not be able to do this alone, especially because I had a full-time job as well.

Thankfully, it was summertime and most of my kids were either home from college or out of school for the summer. I began to delegate. I asked one to research how to bottle-feed a premature goat, another I asked to learn to mix up the powdered milk replacement so that they could do it when I wasn't home, and I asked them each to practice bottle-feeding her so that they could feel confident.

The first few hours went very well, and she seemed to thrive from the milk and the love and attention. However, by the next day, she began to take a turn for the worst. She became much weaker and was unable to keep her eyes open. Her little body became listless. I knew we were at a critical point. I knew we had to pray and pray hard. I began to ask everyone to keep her in their prayers. I was so afraid that she was going to die. She seemed to "hang on." I had been off work during these first few days of caring for her, but I had to return to work soon. I knew this would be a challenge, especially for me to have to leave her and go work a full-time job.

I sat down with my family and asked if they would be willing to take care of her when I was at work and explained that I would take over when I got home every day. They all agreed, but I knew they were afraid that she would die on their watch. I knew I had to remind them that only God is in charge of life and death, and if she didn't make it, it would not be their fault and that God is always in control. As I shared this, I was reminding myself of this as well. You see, I had already become so attached to her.

The first three weeks were very challenging. It felt as if she was barely holding on. I would call home three to four times a day from work and the first thing I would ask was "Is she still alive?" Every morning when I would get up before I looked into her little bed, I would take a deep breath just to prepare myself in case she had passed away during the night. I used a picnic basket as her bed. It was the kind that is seen in old-fashioned movies where the cover has two flaps that fold over the top. The lining was red and white checkered print like a picnic tablecloth. I padded it with soft blankets and stuffed animals placed strategically to support her head and front and back legs, so she wouldn't slide into an uncomfortable position. You see, she was unable to move any part of her body, and if she slid down, she tended to land on her head or neck, placing her at high risk of suffocating.

After the first three weeks, I noticed that she began to respond more and more to us. It was very subtle at first, with eye contact, then she began to wiggle. This wiggling was great cause for celebration! I knew that she was demonstrating potential for progress. I had already told God secretly in my heart that no matter what the outcome was, I would be okay. I had resolved to care for her whether she was totally paralyzed and dependent or not. As an occupational therapist, I had enough background and experience to know what was involved, and I was willing to take this chance. My love for her was so deep that there was no other choice. So her rehabilitation officially began!

I built a partial weight-bearing apparatus out of a coffee can, cloth, broomstick, and two wooden chairs. I placed her in this at least three to four times a day. First, I gently rolled the coffee can back and forth, allowing her feet to "feel" what it was like to put weight through her little legs. I had to position her feet very specifically so that all of her joints were lined up as if she was actually standing. This position was very difficult to maintain because her legs were so weak. This process was very slow. Finally, I began to feel her muscles responding, but they were very small movements. Then she actually began to bob her head up and down ever so slightly. This was a huge improvement! This showed me that she continued to have potential to get better. This was the occupational therapist part of me evaluating her. As time went on, I was able to provide less and less support, especially while feeding her. Then she began communicating with me. I could tell when she wanted me to change her position, when she was hungry, when she needed to use the bathroom, etc. She began to suckle on my earlobe when I carried her, and I could feel without a doubt that she loved me.

One morning, I woke up with the most amazing idea. I was supposed to bring her to work with me!

What? No, no, no! I couldn't, or could I? How would I manage her? How would I do my work and take care of her without it causing chaos or getting her or me sent home?

It was such a strong *feeling* or *prompting* to do this. I was so nervous to even try this. It turned out to be very easy to get approval from my job.

So the day came. I packed our bags. I got a baby carrier. I got the kind that you place over your shoulders and carry the baby next to your chest, and I also brought a knitted purse to wear over one shoulder as a backup plan. I also had baby bottles, milk, and diapers, and off we went!

I put her in the knitted purse first. I was so surprised that hardly anyone even noticed her. If I didn't point her out, I could have gone the whole day without her being discovered. I began to introduce her to my patients. The response was remarkable. It just so happened that on this particular day, I had very grouchy patients. They were usually grouchy due to severe pain, etc. One patient was so grouchy that he had kicked all the other therapists and nurses out of his room. I had a strong *prompting* that he needed to meet Pollyanna.

As I entered his room, I thought, *I really need some help to guide and direct me with this very grouchy man.*

I didn't want him to get more upset because I was bringing a goat into his room. What happened next was so amazing. I walked into his room and showed him my little Pollyanna, and he immediately smiled and asked if he could pet her. I shared with him her life story and all that she had to overcome in her short little life. A tear began to fall from the corner of his eye, and his heart began to melt. He talked of his memories of growing up on a farm with his mom, and how she worked so hard to support him and his brother because his father had died. He explained that his brother had been handicapped, and he remembered feeling sad for his mother for having to work so hard but also felt grateful for her for everything that she had done for him. He missed her terribly even though she had passed away a long time ago. He then stated that he felt he would be dying soon and that he was sorry for being so grouchy, but he was in so much pain and hadn't slept for three days because of it. I asked if he told the nurses about his pain. He said he didn't want to bother them with his complaints.

After he petted Pollyanna, he thanked me so much for bringing her and asked me to please bring her again tomorrow. Of course, I did bring her the next day, and to my surprise, he was smiling when I came to his door. He couldn't wait to tell me that he had slept the night before completely through the night, and his pain was so much better. Although he was feeling better, he continued to say that he knew he would be dying soon. He said he could feel it. As he talked of this, he asked to hold Pollyanna on his lap. She sat so calmly on his lap and leaned up against him as he rubbed her little head. It was as if she knew he needed her. The connection between the two of them was indescribable.

He actually agreed to come out of his room. He had refused to come out of his room for weeks. I pushed him in his wheelchair out into the garden area with Pollyanna resting in his arms. His tears once again fell as he talked of his love for his mother and brother and his regrets for not helping them more. His sadness quickly turned into joy as Pollyanna put her head under his neck and suckled his ear. He thanked me again for bringing her, and he said that he loved her so much and felt that she was like an angel because she made him feel so much better. He was convinced that he had slept better, and his pain went down because he got to visit with her.

When I went to work the following day, I learned that he had died the night before in his sleep. I had a deep *prompting* or *thought* that so much love was brought to this man through Pollyanna, and the timing of his encounter with her enabled him to have some peace and joy and rest and especially less pain. Then I had another *prompting* that if I would continue to bring Pollyanna to work with me, I could reach even more people.

So that is exactly what I started doing. There were so many other examples of Pollyanna helping my patients to heal even as she continued to heal. She began to stand on her feet for at least one to two seconds! This was huge progress! Again, she demonstrated that she had good potential to progress. I began to bring a little "doggie" pen for her. I set her up in the rehab gym. Many times, Pollyanna would try to stand during the same time as the patients were trying to stand during their therapy sessions. The focus became on Pollyanna and her progress, instead of on their own.

Often, the patients could be heard saying these words, "If Pollyanna can do it and keep trying, so can I."

It was not unusual for the other therapists to smile. A smile that acknowledged how much Pollyanna had helped all of these patients. It gently reminded us all of why we actually chose this profession. You see, Pollyanna reached people much deeper than just motivating patients. It seemed almost supernatural. They began to feel connected to her and felt so much love and peace. I continued to share my story of Pollyanna's miraculous journey starting from when she was born. I knew that she was given to me for a reason, and I was beginning to understand why. She knew how much I loved her and that I was going to take good care of her. I could feel when she needed me to change her position, feed her, etc., and she began to know when I was feeling sad and would kiss me on my cheek. This little goat touched more lives in so many ways than I can even count, including my own. I am so thankful for her and that I followed the *prompting* to bring her to work with me. Pollyanna is surely my little miracle.

Lefty the Horse Was in Trouble

. . . .

For as far back as I could remember, I always dreamed of having a horse. It was never a reality when I was a child for many reasons. These were mainly due to living in the suburbs, too much cost, and lack of experience. When I grew up and got married, I shared my dream of having a horse with my late husband. We had some land, but we surely didn't have the money or the experience. As we began to have children, one of my daughters became as interested in having a horse as I had. She was twelve years old.

I would take her with me to drive to an equestrian center where horses were boarded just to have that "feeling" of being around them.

When we would drive through the gates, I would say, "Roll down the windows, so we can enjoy the wonderful smell of the horses!"

As we rolled them down, the most amazing smell would fill our car. We would both take lots of deep breaths and talk of our dream to get a horse one day.

On one of those visits, I met a lady who was giving private horse-riding lessons. I quickly signed my daughter up for this! I couldn't believe it!

At least I could help my daughter learn to ride a horse, I thought.

After a while of taking lessons, we actually met someone who needed to sell their horse.

Could we? I wondered.

We got to meet the horse. His name was "Lefty." On the out-side, he looked like your average brown horse. He even had an old scar on his left knee, but he was far from average. We could feel his spirit as soon as we met him. He was kind and gentle and loving. It felt as if we had been friends forever. My daughter and I both fell in love with him. We daydreamed about being able to buy him and make him a part of our family as we drove home that day. I had big doubts that this would even be possible, but I wanted him so badly.

I sat up that evening with my late husband just watching TV. I wanted to ask him if we could take a chance and buy him. I had already decided that he would be the voice of reason and remind me of why we could not. A long commercial came on, and I took this as an opportunity to bring it up. In the depths of my heart, I wanted this horse. So I began to share about our day at the equestrian center and how we had met a horse that was for sale. He was listening, but I thought he was only listening halfway, waiting for the TV show to come back on. To my surprise, he turned off the TV and gave me his full attention. As I began to talk about Lefty, I got more and more excited. I shared that we had already had a chance to ride him and that he was so gentle and followed our directions so well!

My husband gave me the biggest surprise by responding with "Well, let's go see him together and see if we can make him a part of our family."

I couldn't believe it! I was so happy that he would even consider it!

The next day, I met him at the equestrian center after work. When I got there, I was shocked to see my late husband riding Lefty across the pasture! He came up to us with the biggest smile!

"Let's get him!" my late husband said.

Lefty quickly became ours and we became his. He seemed so happy to be a part of our family. He fit in with all the other ani-mals on our little farm. He especially became very close with our goats. One particular goat named St. Francis quickly became his best friend, and they were inseparable. The adventure quickly began. My daughter began to ride him the most, and she would just get on him bareback and would even lay on him backward, and he would just walk around the property gently, and they would just spend quiet afternoons together. My favorite thing to do with Lefty was to sit with him. I would bring my plastic chair outside and position it right next to him so that we would be facing each other. His head would hang down and rest almost in my lap, and I would put my face next to his, and I could smell his sweet breath and he could feel mine too. Often, he would stay in this position until his eyes would gently close, and he would fall asleep like this. I remember feeling as if I never wanted to move. It was so comforting. I loved him so, and I knew he loved me.

After a few years, he began to show signs of a little pain in his left knee. A veterinarian said it was arthritis and gave us some topical medication. During this time, we had some big challenges in our family. One of them was a very scary diagnosis of nasopharyngeal cancer for my husband. This was his second bout with cancer. His first cancer diagnosis was testicular cancer when he was nineteen years old. This was devastating for our family. We began a long journey of chemotherapy and radiation for him that resulted in him losing almost one hundred pounds. I was so focused on keeping him alive and overcoming this cancer that I hadn't realized that Lefty's knee had become more painful, and he had started having difficulty walking at times.

One evening, which happened to be a particularly difficult day of chemotherapy, after finally getting my late husband comfortable and his pain somewhat under control, I decided to go out and check on Lefty. I couldn't believe what I found. Lefty was down on the ground in the front yard. At first, I thought maybe he was just resting comfortably on the freshly cut lawn. As I got closer, I noticed that his left knee was swollen, and he was unable to stand up by himself. My heart sank. I knew how important it is to make sure horses don't stay lying on the ground for too long, so I tried to coax him up. He could barely lift his head. I continued to try and try. I tried to pull him up using a lead rope, and he could just barely lift his head. Then I tried to push him from the back just to give him a cue to try to stand up. I pushed and pushed, becoming more and more dirty and muddy and covered in sweat. He didn't even budge.

By this time, it had become nighttime and very dark. My late husband was in no condition to help me. I finally got a hold of my daughter, and she was on her way home from soccer practice. I was alone outside in the dark with Lefty who was definitely in trouble. I was scared. I decided to sit with him. I sat down on the wet grass next to his head. There had been a gentle rain earlier that day, and the grass was still wet. I reached out and touched his face, rubbing his cheeks and his forehead. I put my face next to his so that I could once again smell his sweet breath and so that he could feel mine. I knew that this gave comfort to me, and I was hoping that it would do the same for him.

I then began to rub his shoulders, chest, and belly. I could see he was breathing comfortably, but I was so worried.

How can I get him up? I thought.

I couldn't hold back the tears. I was so sad for my late husband and his cancer, and I was so sad for Lefty. I felt so helpless to take care of both of them. I remembered how my late husband had so willingly made it possible for us to even buy Lefty and bring him home, and I was so thankful. He had made my dream of having a horse come true, and now I was trying to balance between caring for my husband and caring for Lefty.

I sat up on my knees and leaned over Lefty, placing my arms around him to give him a big hug. My heart was so very sad. I started talking to him. I told him how much I loved him and explained that he needed to get up or that he might get stuck there. I began to have a *prompting* or a *gut feeling* to place my hands on his knee. I began to beg God deep in my heart to heal him. Also, I had heard that horses have a kind of "sixth sense" and could sort of read our minds, so I decided to try something. I began to talk to Lefty in my mind, and I asked him to get up. I continued to keep one hand on his knee, and I placed the other hand on his heart.

After just a few minutes, Lefty actually lifted his head. Then to my surprise, he tried to sit up or prop himself into a more upright position! I continued to keep my hands in place and to talk to Lefty and to God in my mind. Just as my daughter came pulling up to the driveway, Lefty actually tried to stand up! It took at least five attempts and some strategic positioning of his legs, but as my daughter came running over to us, Lefty had made it into an upright standing position! His legs were shaking, but he was standing up!

What had just happened? I thought. *Had Lefty actually heard me? Did God hear my secret prayer? What had made Lefty try to stand up right at that moment? Why did I get the prompting to place my hands on him and to try to send him mental messages? What if I had missed the promptings and just given up on him?*

My daughter and I were so happy to see him standing up that we began to jump up and down and then we took him on a walk around the property to help his legs get used to walking again. He was walking just fine with no signs of pain or weakness. It was truly amazing. So many things could have gone wrong if he had stayed down on the ground.

As soon as we put him up in the barn, we began to get a terrible thunderstorm.

What if Lefty was still lying on the ground in all this rain? I thought.

I went back into the house to check on my late husband, and I found him sleeping very comfortably with no signs of pain. He hadn't even known what I was dealing with outside with Lefty. He was too sick to have helped me anyway. As I laid down on the bed next to him, I wrapped my arms around his waist, and I felt such thankfulness for that moment of peace and for him being comfortable. I knew that what had just happened with Lefty was a miracle. It was a true miracle. It may not seem like a big thing to others, but in my heart, I knew that I had witnessed something that was supernatural. It was a message to me that miracles do happen. I couldn't explain how Lefty knew to try to stand up just when I was asking him to and when I had asked God for help. As my arms were embracing my late husband, I asked God to help him too. This day had also been a message to me to not give up. I decided to just be thankful for this day and not worry about tomorrow. I told myself that I would continue to believe that my late husband would recover and get better. I was so thankful, and I kissed him good night.

Peanut the Sheep Saves the Day

- - - - - - - - -

We have this wonderful sheep who we call Peanut. He is multicolored with many shades of brown. I must admit that I have had many pet sheep in my life, but he is by far the sweetest and kindest sheep I have ever had. It might have something to do with how he came to be part of our family.

One day many years ago, my late husband was driving along and noticed a sheep with a long rope wandering right down the middle of the highway. He automatically pulled over to try to coax the sheep out of the busy intersection. He opened the door of our minivan to try to find a leash or another rope to try to harness him, so he would at least be safe and out of harm's way and, of course, not cause a car accident. Instead, the sheep followed him and actually jumped right inside of the van and wouldn't get out!

My late husband called me and said, "Hun, a sheep just jumped into the van, and I can't get him out!"

I couldn't help but laugh. It sounded so absurd and unbelievable. He went on to explain that he was going to stop by the neighboring houses and ask if he belonged to anyone. No one claimed him. We put up flyers that same day, and for at least two weeks, we tried to find his owner. No one stepped up for him. We, of course, took care of him while we looked for his owner. He was so sweet and a little shy. He loved getting his back scratched and petted behind his ears. He began to follow me all around the farm and quickly made friends with the other animals, especially with my little dwarf Nigerian goats. They loved him, and he loved all of them.

I soon noticed that I could hear Peanut making his "*baa*" sounds. I didn't pay much attention to it, but one day, I really took notice that his "*baa*" sounds sounded very curious. He was making this sound over and over and over. It began to sound as if he was actually calling me. I decided to go outside and investigate. The sound was coming from way far back at the end of the property in the farthest pasture. I had to walk through some very high pasture grass in order to follow his sound.

I finally made it to the back, and I saw him pacing back and forth. As soon as he saw me, he ran up to me then he appeared to toss his head back and forth as if to somehow point toward a certain direction.

Could he be trying to tell me something? I thought. *How could this be? Can sheep really communicate like this?* I wondered.

I tried to follow where I thought Peanut was trying to get me to go. I had to walk further into very high and thick shrubs and overgrown sticker bushes. All of a sudden, I saw something. It looked like one of my small dwarf Nigerian goats, but it looked like she was trapped or caught on the fence. As I got even closer, I saw that it was my little goat named Olive. She was, in fact, caught on the fence, only she was hanging upside down by her hooves! She was hanging by her two back legs with the wire of the fencing somehow wrapped around her two tiny, little hooves. She wasn't making a sound. I wasn't even sure that she was alive. She was hanging there limp.

I raced over to her and tried to lift her up at least a little, and I noticed that she was at least breathing. I wondered how long she had been hanging there. She must be so scared and in pain. I tried and tried to get her loose, but I just couldn't. I had forgotten my cell phone. I always carried it with me, but for some reason, I had forgotten it this time. I yelled and yelled for help, and finally, my son heard me. He was able to find some wire cutters, and with much effort, he and I were able to coordinate lifting her up and cutting her loose from the wire. I was so afraid that it had cut into her little legs, but after examining her, she didn't have any cuts or gashes. She seemed very tired, and I could feel her heart beating through her chest. As I carried her, I hugged her tightly and whispered into her ear that I loved her so much and that she was safe, and I told her that I was so sorry that this had happened.

I took her to be with her mom and the rest of the goat herd. As I placed her down, she was able to stand on all four feet and then began to walk. She then ran easily toward her mom with no signs of pain or injury. I watched her in amazement feeling so thankful that we were able to get her out of that terrible situation. Then I remembered that it was all because of Peanut!

It all started with him crying to me for help. How had he known to do that? How did he know that she was in trouble, and how did he know to call? As I thought back, I remember that his calling was repetitive and sounded urgent and almost frantic. I almost missed this. I almost didn't pay attention to his calling. I could have so easily missed it if I had been too busy or thinking about other things, etc. This precious sheep that we had rescued in turn found a way to rescue another. How amazing this was! I was so incredibly thankful!

I sat with Peanut and scratched his back and rubbed his ears just as I knew he loved, and I thanked him from the bottom of my heart. I told him that he was the hero that day. I also told him that I was sorry that it took me so long to come, and if he needed me again that I would pay very close attention to him and his calling.

I knew from that day forward that he was my farm guardian and my informant with anything that might go wrong on the farm. He has definitely fulfilled that role, and I have lots and lots of situations in which he has saved other animals or let me know when they broke out of the fence or even if a stranger is standing by the front gate looking into my pasture. He is such a special boy, and I love him so much, but I am especially thankful for the *promptings* that I had that day to save my little goat Olive.

The Cat and the Baby Bird

One morning, I got up early to make my coffee. I was feeling extra tired from a very long night of taking care of my late husband. He had been diagnosed with stomach cancer. This was now his third time to have cancer. He was having an especially difficult time with his chemotherapy treatment.

I really needed that coffee. I was more than just tired. I was utterly exhausted. I grew up hearing my grandmother say, "I feel like I've been run over by a Mack truck," but I never understood what she meant until now. I knew my fatigue was physical but probably more emotional. The sadness and worry had become all-consuming. I was so worried that he was going to die from this, and I didn't know how to keep this from happening. I had spent so much time trying to research and think of anything and everything that I could possibly do to make him better. As I stood over the kitchen sink, I looked out the window. I saw something moving far out in the backyard, but I couldn't make it out. I blinked and blinked, trying to clear the morning blurriness out of my eyes. Finally, my eyes began to focus, and I could finally see what I was actually looking at.

It was our cat "Lilly" who had caught a tiny, little, very delicate baby bird. The cat was playing with it. She actually had the little thing in between her two front paws and was batting her back and forth. Then she would let the bird get away just a little bit, then she would pounce on her and begin batting her back and forth again between her paws.

Poor little thing! I've got to save her! I thought.

I raced to put on my rubber boots at the back door, and I began to run so fast that I ended up jumping off the last three steps, almost landing flat on my face. That slowed me down just enough to look at the cat again. I knew that I had to have a plan; or the cat would run away with this little bird in her mouth, and I would lose my chance to save her. I decided to get a piece of cheese to try to bribe that cat away from the bird. I wasn't even sure if the bird was injured. I had to get her away from this cat. It took a while to get the cat's attention with the cheese. She attempted to sniff the cheese and seemed interested in it at first, but then quickly turned her nose up at it and went right back to "playing," or what I call torturing this little bird. I went back into the house for something that the cat would not be able to refuse. I opened up a can of tuna.

I tried again. I walked up to the cat, trying to be very sweet, making all the "*meow*" noises, and she got a whiff of the tuna smell. Soon, she dropped the little bird. I placed the tuna can down and tried to grasp the bird as the cat went toward the lure of the tuna. I could see that the bird was indeed injured. She was having trouble flying and was trying to hop away to somewhere safe. I tried to catch her before the cat came back. Although she was injured, she was able to hop fast enough to elude my grip. I'm sure she was already traumatized from the cat and saw me as an enemy too. She hopped into a big bushy area. I tried to grab her before she got into the bush, but I was too late. I wanted to at least make sure that she wasn't hurt too badly. We had one veterinarian in town that actually helped birds. My plan was to try to catch her and take her to the doctor if she needed it. I was on a mission to save her. There was so much mud underneath that bush, but I didn't even care.

I squatted down on my hands and knees, and I got as close as I could. It took me many, many tries to reach in for her, but finally after what felt like a very long time, I was actually able to pick her up. I had her in the palm of my hand. As I brought her close to me, I was able to get a really good look at her. She was so much smaller than I had realized. I could feel her heart beating. I knew she must be so scared. Right at that moment, I saw a bird that looked just like her but much bigger, flying right above me. I wondered if it could be her mother. I watched the bird fly to a nearby tree. I decided to place this little bird near the base of that tree to see what would happen. Meanwhile, I grabbed Lilly the cat and took her into the house and fed her again.

I wanted to give the bird a chance to hopefully find her family first before I tried to interfere too much more. I watched them from afar. That bird that flew over me did in fact go next to this little one. She seemed to hover over her. I really think she was the momma bird. After a little while, they both just flew together up into the tree. I just stood there in amazement. I was so thankful that she was okay enough to fly and that another bird seemed to have helped her get to safety. Then I had a *thought* or a *prompting* deep down in my heart.

I could hear "That little bird is you, and I know you feel like life is batting you back and forth between its paws just like it did to that little bird. You are not alone. If I can send help for this little one, I can send help for you too. Please don't give up."

This *thought* or *prompting* was so incredibly strong, and I knew it was just for me. I needed some kind of encouragement, any kind of encouragement, today of all days. I was feeling so defeated.

As I stood there thinking about this message that I knew was just exactly what I needed to hear today, I realized that I could have so easily missed it. I could have missed all of it. It had all started by me stumbling to the kitchen, desperate for a cup of coffee, feeling so exhausted. But I had felt the *prompting*. The prompting for all of this, to look out of the window, to try to save the bird, how to distract the cat, how to even catch the bird, and finally to just be still and watch the momma bird take care of this little one and then, of course, the message that was intended just for me. I was so thankful that I had heard the prompting and, most importantly, that I had listened to it. My mind began to race with the thought that there must be so many other opportunities like this one all around us.

I took a deep breath in thankfulness. I decided that I would try to pay closer attention so that I could learn to hear these more clearly.

Lefty and the Baby Chick

I always knew that our horse Lefty was a unique horse with a kind and sweet spirit, but what I didn't realize was that I was underestimating his ability for empathy.

One very rainy and cloudy winter afternoon, I found myself walking around outside seemingly checking on all of my farm animals, but in reality, I was walking to try to calm my emotions. My late husband had been diagnosed with nasopharyngeal cancer. I was so worried. He was losing a lot of weight, and it had recently become very hard for him to eat anything. My escape was to go outside and walk and spend time with my animals. I was scared. It felt as if the world was crashing down on me, and I didn't know what to do or how to stop it.

As soon as I started walking around the pasture, Lefty saw me. Before I even realized it, he had made his way to me. As I turned to go to see my chickens, Lefty followed me. I loved it when he followed me. It was so comforting especially when I was feeling sad or emotional, and today was definitely one of those days. As I was walking through the pasture, I saw one of my chickens just sitting in the grass, and I noticed that her wings and feathers were kind of fluffy. Then all of a sudden, she stood up and at least twelve very tiny newborn baby chickens started running out from underneath her. They were so incredibly cute! I was so mesmerized by how tiny and adorable they were that I didn't notice that Lefty came walking right up next me, right into the area of all these babies.

Mama chickens usually become so protective of their babies that they can actually become aggressive but not this one. She trusted me and she loved me, and she knew that I loved her. I squatted down to get a better look at her babies, and she graciously let me. It seemed that she was even proud of them and wanted to show them off to me as she walked around, checking on each one and showing them how to look on the ground for bugs. I was happily distracted by all of them.

I was so distracted that I hadn't noticed that Lefty was walking closer and closer to these little babies. He started doing what he usually did when I came outside and especially when I would squat down. He pushed his way up against me with his head, which was his way of asking for love and scratches behind his ears and on his nose. He loved this. He was a very affectionate horse. He would let me love on him all day if I wanted to. So I reached over and rubbed his face and behind his ears. He continued to come closer and closer, and I gave in to his requests. I loved and needed it too, especially today.

All of a sudden, I had a *prompting* or a *gut feeling* that something was not right. I decided to stand up.

Oh my gosh! The babies are walking around Lefty's feet! I thought.

The baby chicks had walked so close to Lefty that they were all around his four feet. I had to act fast! I tried to shoo them out from under him, but they kept walking around his feet in circles. I could get one or two of them away, but the others would go right into the "danger zone," right next to his very large hooves. The mama chicken was distracted with hunting for bugs and didn't realize that anything was wrong. I began to get very worried that Lefty would step on them. It was a real possibility! Those babies were all around his feet! I thought about throwing some chicken food away from the area, and hopefully, the mama chicken would follow me and thus babies would follow her.

This almost worked, but one of the babies remained underneath Lefty. I rushed back to try to grab her. At the same time, Lefty decided to follow me too. He wanted some of that chicken food. I hadn't thought of that. I rushed to grab that little chick that was next to his feet. As I reached down, the baby ran right underneath his foot, and Lefty's foot went down right on top of her as well.

Oh no! She is crushed for sure! I thought.

I didn't even want to check. My heart sank, and I felt so sick in my stomach.

I was already feeling emotional, and now I just felt defeated. I started to cry. Lefty put his head on my shoulder, and I could feel his warm breath against my face. I knew he wanted to comfort me. It wasn't his fault that he had stepped on the baby chick. He was such a large animal; it was bound to happen. How could he even know that these little ones were underneath him. What I didn't know was that he was trying to tell me something. He dropped his head down close to the ground. I glanced down as he did this, and he looked at me. Then he lifted his head. Then the next thing that happened was totally astounding. He lifted his left hoof. This was the hoof that had stepped on the baby chick. As he lifted his hoof, out ran the baby chick!

"How was that little chick even alive? How did that little chick even survive being stepped on by a two thousand-pound animal?"

She ran out toward her mother and began to hunt and peck for bugs like all of her other brothers and sisters as if nothing bad had even happened.

I looked at Lefty, and he looked at me. I absolutely couldn't believe what I had just witnessed. I loved on Lefty and told him thank you for being so gentle with the baby. I trusted him to be kind and loving, and even though he was this huge animal, he was so gentle. My heart felt so happy that she had not been squashed and killed.

Then I had another *prompting*. This time, it was an awareness, an awareness of what all of this had really meant. When I first came outside to walk, I was feeling like the world was crashing down on me. I felt defeated, like I was being squashed with no way out.

As I replayed what had happened to this little baby chick, I could hear deep inside my heart, "The baby chick represents me, and Lefty's foot represents God's protection, not the world. And if I will just trust this, this weight will soon be lifted. For now I will be covered and protected, not crushed."

I was so humbled by this message from this *prompting*. I knew that it was just for me at this moment in time to help me with the painful despair that I had been feeling. I could have so easily missed all of this if I had been caught up or distracted in my own life and my own pain. It all started with Lefty, his loving nature, newborn baby chicks, and ultimately watching a metaphor of my life unfold right before my eyes in real time. I was so humbled.

Little Miracle Kitten

● ● ● ● ● ●

S everal years before my late husband passed away, he had felt a strong prompting to go to help the homeless or houseless and provide them a hot meal, along with words of encouragement about hope and about God. This had become a great *calling* for him. We began to go every Sunday, rain or shine. We had an opportunity to help many people, but the best part was actually getting to know them on a personal level. They shared many things with us about their lives and their struggles and sometimes even their victories. We got to see some who finally found places to live, jobs, and even reunited with their families. We had become friends with many of them. This is not to say that we didn't have our challenges though. There were some people who were not so nice and friendly. My late husband was always kind and knew how to resolve issues peacefully.

On one particular day, we found ourselves taking down the tables after providing a hot meal, and I was prompted to turn around behind me. As I did, I couldn't help but see a man who frequently came to eat with us. He had always been very nice and friendly, but today he looked as if he was having a very bad day. He began to yell loudly and was very frustrated. I continued to feel prompted to focus on him and to even go a little closer. I normally would have removed myself from this just to be safe. As I continued to pay attention to him, something caught my eye. He was holding a very tiny kitten. It looked to be only two or three weeks old. As I looked closer, I noticed it had a rope tied around it like a makeshift harness.

As I was watching this man, he began to get upset with this kitten. He grabbed her and held her up to his face and began to scream and shake her! My heart sank. I wanted so badly to take it from him, but he was getting more and more volatile. My late husband was very far on the other side from me and had no idea what was going on. Actually, no one else was near me at the time.

Then this distraught man actually caught me looking at him. We made eye contact.

I thought, *Oh no! He sees me and now he is going to get mad at me too!*

I stayed very still and held my breath. I said a little prayer in my heart for me and the kitten, but I was prompted to stay right there and not leave.

He walked right up to me, yelling and screaming at this kitten and then threw her down to the ground forcefully right at my feet, screaming, "You take her! I don't want her anymore! I'm done with her forever!"

Then he ran off down the street. I looked at the tiny kitten, and I knew I had to act fast. I tried to ignore my fear and think on my feet on how to catch her. I knew she was terrified and would probably run away. I wanted to hold her and love her and especially make sure that she wasn't injured. I saw some of the rope that was tied around her trailing behind, and I quickly stepped on it. At the same time, she tried to run away. Thankfully, I got to the rope first. Then I slowly and gently reached down and scooped her up into my hands. She was so tiny that she fit into my palm. I couldn't help but notice how much she was shaking and crying in total fear. I also noticed that this rope was tied so tightly around her chest and neck. I knew she must be so hungry and thirsty. Right at that moment, I had at least three people run up to me and tell me that they were so thankful that I had been the one to rescue her and that he had been treating her this way all morning, but they were too scared to try to take her away. We were actually just packing up the last of our supplies, so I raced to my late husband and showed him the kitten and briefly told him what happened.

He also felt sad for her. We drove straight to the store to get her something to eat. He held her while I went to look for milk and some soft kitten food. As I came out, I saw him holding her next to his chest, and she seemed to have slowed down a bit from the shaking but was still crying. I poured some milk into a tiny little container. She began to drink the milk. She drank it as if she hadn't had anything to drink for days and days.

She drank four refills of milk. She continued to cry all the while she was drinking. I wondered if she was in pain. Then I opened the small can of food. She began to eat and eat. I couldn't believe how much she was drinking and eating. She continued to cry even as she was eating. She finally stopped eating and curled up into my hand. I pressed her against my chest as we drove home. I took her inside, and I decided to lay down and continue to hold her close to me. I showed her to my son, and he quickly grabbed some scissors and helped me remove that rope. It was very difficult to cut off. It was tied around her much more tightly than I had even realized. I began to whisper to her that I was so sorry that this had happened to her and that she was safe now and that I would take care of her. I told her she had a new home now. It was amazing. As soon as I told her those things, she stopped crying. I could feel her little body begin to relax against mine, and she fell asleep. She slept on my chest for quite a long time. I didn't dare move because I didn't want to wake her.

Later, after she did wake up, she began to try to walk around a little. She seemed to be okay. I was able to take a good look at her for any injuries or painful areas. Surprisingly, she seemed fine. She began to act somewhat like a normal little kitten. She was so very small. I got her a little blanket and placed it right next to my side of the bed. She was so smart. She knew it was for her. We became so close, and at night, I would wake up to find that she had crawled up into my bed and was sleeping on my chest soundly, even purring at times. I knew she felt safe, secure, and especially loved. She was part of our family now.

When she got old enough, I got her spayed, and she began to venture outside to follow me to feed and milk my goats! This cat became my milking partner. She sits with me as I milk my goats, and I can actually squirt the milk in her direction, and she will drink it! She is so precious! I gave her the name Gracie.

I knew that the *promptings* that I had felt on the day we met were so powerful and enabled me to save her and bring her home to be part of our family. I was so thankful to that man for placing her at my feet. Of all the people he could have done that to, I knew I was the best one because I have such a love and compassion for all animals. I would have done anything to try to save her. I was so glad that if he had to give her away to someone, it was me.

Her name represents grace. And we all need to give each other grace. I remember thinking that I could have so easily missed this opportunity to have saved her if I had ignored those *promptings* or the *gut feelings* to really pay attention to that distraught man and notice that he was actually holding this tiny little precious creature. I realized that she was actually "brought" to me and placed at my feet. This may seem like a small thing, but to me, how it all unfolded seemed supernatural. I hope I can continue to listen to the *promptings* and notice more moments like this. I wanted to learn so much more from these types of encounters.

Water Tank Fiasco

L ately, I've been thinking about how I've been learning to listen to the *promptings* or my *gut feelings*. As I reflect, I realize that actually I've been hearing them for years. I just didn't realize what they were, or that they even had any meaning or substance.

Recently, I had to go outside and check on my water catchment tank to make sure we had enough water. I live in a rural area in Hawaii, and this type of system is how we get our water to our house for bathing, washing, dishes, etc. The water is caught from the roof using the gutters to direct the water into a large cistern or above-the-ground water catchment tank. We've been living with this type of system for years, and I actually really like it. It means we do not have a water bill, and it also makes us understand and appreciate water, and we have learned how to conserve it. It has been a great lesson for my kids as well. This area in Hawaii is very environmentally conscious. Even our garbage and trash set up for our county requires that we haul our own trash to the dump, which they call it a transfer station, and we have to separate it such as green waste, cardboard, metal, etc.

So as I was outside checking on my water level in my tank, I had a *prompting* or thought. It was so strong, and I was literally brought back in time with a very strong memory. This memory was at least twenty-five years ago when I only had my first two children, and they were ages three and five years old. I could see them in my mind as if it was yesterday. It was a very warm and beautiful sunny afternoon, and I had been outside in my backyard with my two little girls. They were playing near me as I hung out the sheets and blankets on the clothesline to dry. They were playing in the grass with their little dolls sliding on their little plastic slide. Our water tank was nearby. I went inside for a few moments to get more laundry. I was always very protective of them, but I felt confident to go inside for a moment because I could see them from my back door and my kitchen window.

Our home was built on a design called post and pier, which meant it was up off the ground about four feet, so there was an area underneath the house enabling one to reach the plumbing etc., and it had stairs to enter the front and back door. I decided since I could see them from my kitchen window, that I would just go ahead and wash the dishes in the sink and put a casserole in the oven. So that is what I did.

As I began to do these chores, I started having a bad feeling. I couldn't place what it was, but that feeling continued to linger in my mind. Although I could easily see the girls from the kitchen window, I went to the door and looked right outside and checked on the girls a little closer. They were perfectly fine and having so much fun playing together. As I headed back to the kitchen sink to finish the dishes, I had a strong prompting to make the girls come inside the house. This feeling became very strong to the point of overwhelming. I immediately went outside and told them to follow me back inside the house. They both didn't want to and tried to talk me into letting them stay. I told them that they had to come inside. My five-year-old continued to ask why. I couldn't give her a reason, but I felt that it was urgent. I actually grasped both of their hands to guide them into the house. My three-year-old decided to throw a little temper tantrum, so I had to let go of her hand and actually pick her up.

I grasped my five-year-old and said in a firm voice, "We have to go inside now!"

She did not argue.

As I was walking into the back door, I had several fleeting thoughts. First, I thought that I must be overreacting. Why was I feeling so strongly to get the kids inside? Then I remembered that "Scarlet," my black cocker spaniel, was outside, and I had seen her sleeping underneath the house. I quickly became distracted with the kids complaining about having to come inside, so I tried to find them something else to play with. As soon as I got them settled, I went back to washing my dishes.

All of a sudden, I heard the loudest noise that sounded like an explosion coming from the backyard! I couldn't even imagine what it could be! I headed for the back door to take a look outside. As I opened the door, all I could see was crazy, huge waves of water rushing toward the very steps that I was standing on!

"How in the world is this even happening? Where is this water even coming from?"

My mouth dropped open in shock. My parents had just arrived from the mainland for a visit that day and had been resting in the back room to sleep off their jetlag.

They came running down the hall, yelling, "What is that terrible noise?"

As I watched the water continue to flow, wave after wave, I couldn't find the words to even answer them. They came up alongside me, and we watched in utter disbelief. As the water finally went down, I saw that our water tank had somehow exploded. It had broken apart and that is where all of the water had come from. Thousands of gallons of water.

Right at that moment, I saw my little dog Scarlett come walking out from underneath the house, soaking wet from the water, and walking slowly. She meandered her way up to the top of the steps and came inside. I rushed to hug her and then I grabbed a towel and dried her off.

My mind began to race. *My poor dog could have drowned!* I thought. *Oh my gosh! My children!* Then I remembered!

My little girls were just outside in that same area! What if I hadn't insisted that they come inside. What if I hadn't had that strong *feeling* or *prompting* to make them come inside. They would have literally been swept underneath the house and actually could have been severely injured or even killed.

At that moment, my heart began to pound so hard my chest actually hurt. I looked at my parents, and they looked at me. We all just had that same realization. I grabbed my girls and hugged them so tightly that they had to ask me to stop because it was so tight, they couldn't breathe. I didn't want to let go of them, not then, not ever. I knew we had just escaped a very dangerous and crazy situation. No one could have predicted this would happen. It was a very rare thing to happen. No one we asked had even ever heard of such a thing happening. It was determined that the man who built it for us must have used the wrong thickness of material for the size and diameter and that the pressure from the water was too great. Whatever the reason, I was so thankful that I had that *feeling* to bring them inside, and most importantly, I acted on that feeling to bring them inside even though I didn't understand why I was doing it.

Even though it was so long ago, and my girls are all grown up now, I know that this was the *prompting* or *gut feeling* that I am learning about now at this time in my life. I am so thankful.

The Driving Force of Fear

I've been really wanting to learn more and more about really looking and listening for the *promptings* or *gut feelings* that can guide and direct us and provide some kind of direction with this thing called life.

On one particular day, I was heavy in thought. Mainly about my late husband before he died. It was at a time where he was dealing with his fourth cancer, which was stomach cancer. He was very sick and weak and had lost a lot of weight. I was working so hard to take care of him and provide the extra care that he needed for just basic activities of daily living. I was also doing the heavy chores around the house. These were quite labor intensive because we live in a very rural area. We have to haul our own garbage and collect our own drinking water from a spring well. It is usually not that hard, and I usually enjoy it, but today seemed extra hard because I was so worried about my late husband. He wasn't doing very well at all. I was also trying to keep working at my job, so we could continue to pay the bills. I was feeling very tired and very overwhelmed.

As I struggled to keep up with all of these chores, I couldn't help but notice that my dogs began to bark frantically. I decided to go outside and look to see what was going on. I could see them barking, but I couldn't see what they were barking at. I had to go outside and walk way out toward the back of our three-acre property. Far back against the edge of the property is a forest, and that is where the dogs were barking. As I walked toward the forest line, I saw what they were barking at! It was a huge wild pig, and because of its very large tusks, I figured it was a boar. I couldn't believe how big it was!

Immediately, I became afraid for my dogs as well as for myself but especially for my dogs. I could tell that they were trying to protect me as well as their home. Wild pigs have recently become a big problem in our area due to lots of new building and clearing going on all around us. One boar had broken into my pigpen with my two female potbellied pigs and impregnated them. I ended up with twenty-nine baby piglets running all over my land. That is another story all by itself. As I looked at this, what I considered a very dangerous situation, I began to remember another situation that happened a very long time ago.

I had my first two babies at that time, ages one and three years old. I had decided to go for a nice long walk down our road using my stroller. We live in a very rural, country type area with dirt roads. Back then we hardly had any neighbors with maybe three or four houses on our entire street. Today, we have practically every lot with new homes being built. As I went for my walk, I felt very safe and confident. Cell phones were not even in existence yet. I grabbed up a big stick and felt that it was good enough for me if I needed it. I ended up walking a little farther down my road than I had planned, mainly because it was such a nice day, and we were enjoying it. All of a sudden, as if from out of nowhere, this very mean and aggressive dog came charging down from one of the homes, turned the corner, and came running and barking straight for us! We were all alone out there except for this mad and crazy dog. It was literally running straight for us, and I could see his snarling teeth from afar. My heart began to pound out of my chest. I had two small babies in my stroller and really no way to defend myself.

My thoughts began to race. *What if this dog attacked me? What would happen to my babies? What if he attacked my babies? How would I get help?*

I knew with each second, I was getting closer to a very awful and intensely dangerous situation. I took a deep breath and said a quiet prayer for help deep inside of my heart. All of a sudden, I had a thought or what I now know as a *prompting*. I had to stand up to this dog. I couldn't run and hide. I had to face him head on. The thought or feeling was so strong. I just sprang into action. I jumped right in front of my stroller, getting between the dog and my babies. Then I remember just following my *gut feeling* to make myself look as big and strong as I could, posturing my body as if I was some kind of huge bodybuilder or wrestler or something, flexing my arm muscles while yelling as loud as I could, sounding like a huge growl, and staring that dog right in the eyes. I didn't back down, and I continued to hold my ground. As soon as I "growled" as loudly as I could and gave him my most intense stare, that dog stopped, looked me back in the eye, and then actually turned and tucked his tail, and ran back to where he had come from.

I remember thinking at that point, *What just happened? Had I scared that ferocious crazy dog?*

I was so thankful but very shaken up by the whole thing. I turned around and headed home as fast as I could go. My babies really didn't even know what had happened. They seemed happy and unaware. I was incredibly thankful.

After I had gotten home, it took me a very long time to stop shaking, but I remember thinking, *How in the world did I know to do that?*

Today as I learn about following the *promptings*, I can recognize it more easily. I know that I had a *prompting* or *gut feeling* to stand up to that dog, and it most definitely saved all of our lives. As I stand here looking at this crazy wild pig and reflect on that crazy dog story from long ago, I also recognize that *promptings* come in different ways and that, today, the *prompting* has come in the form of this memory.

Oh boy! I thought. *Do I have to do this again?*

I took another deep breath and, again, said another quiet prayer deep inside my heart. I felt that *prompting*. I knew what I needed to do. I had my doubts though. It seemed very dangerous, and I wouldn't recommend anyone to try this. But at this point, I was too close to the wild pig, and he had already seen me. I was in immediate danger, and I couldn't run. I had no weapon either. Again, I stood as big and strong as I could, flexing my arm muscles, and I yelled out the biggest growl I possibly could belt out. I also stared at him. I knew that he could actually kill me and my two dogs if he really wanted to. In that split moment, I also thought of my late husband and wondered what would happen to him if I was badly injured or worse. I had to stay focused, and I kept repeating my quiet prayer for help.

To my surprise, that wild pig looked right at me and paused. He didn't move. Then after what felt like a lifetime, which was really only maybe a minute, he turned and ran right back into the forest where he had come from. I called my dogs to me so that they wouldn't follow him there. Thank goodness they listened to my instructions. I relaxed my strained muscles and actually leaned forward and rested my hands on my knees, taking a huge deep breath.

What in the world just happened? I thought. *Had I actually done it again?*

I knew that I knew, that I had definitely heard or felt the *prompting* to do this. I am usually very fearful of any type of danger-ous confrontation, and I know I would not have thought to do this long ago, or even now, to handle this situation. With both situations, I had been given some kind of supernatural help, and I knew the promptings were the guiding force behind them.

As I began to get my breath back, I started reflecting on what had happened. The basic situation was amazing itself but then I got another thought or *prompting*. I could hear deep in my heart that this was also symbolic of fear, fear with anything. I was reminded that I was facing my own fears. These fears included losing my husband to cancer, not being able to pay my bills because I couldn't work and take care of him at the same time, etc., and on and on. The *prompt-ings* continued with emphasis on "knowing" that the physical process of "standing up" to my fear after saying that quiet prayer for help is what I need to do with all of my fears. It was a metaphor for me. It also helped me recognize how much fear I was actually having about the possibility of losing my late husband to his illness and worrying so much about the whole process and the all-encompassing fear of being left alone and the total sadness that continued to fall on me. I was amazed at how I had wanted so desperately to learn more and more about how to hear or see these *promptings*, and today, it seemed that I had been taken to a whole new level of learning. I really could see how it was beginning to all make sense, and how the crazy "coincidental" chain of events actually was helping guide me through this next chapter in my life.

Ester and the Eggs

I have this sweet little potbellied pig named Ester, who just happens to have been born with deformed hind legs. She doesn't know that she is different from the other pigs. She has been able to overcome her challenges and has taught herself to walk. When I watch her walk, I am always reminded of how long it took her to learn to walk. She is an inspiration and gently reminds me that if she can overcome her challenges of badly deformed legs and learn to walk on them, then I can surely overcome any of my challenges or hardships.

She is all grown up now and has made friends with all the other animals on my little farm. She has especially befriended the chickens. They seem to really love her, and she loves them. I notice this especially at feeding time and when they settle down to go to sleep at night. Pigs are known for their gluttonous behavior especially when eating and have been known to be aggressive around food. Ester has none of these qualities. She is very willing to share her food with the other chickens, and she is so gentle around them.

One afternoon as I was outside checking on all the animals, I was *prompted* to look for Ester. I couldn't find her anywhere. I began to get a little worried. Ester knew her name and always came to me when I called her. I walked all over the farm calling for her. My worry began to turn into fear. I didn't know if maybe she had gotten out or if someone had actually broken in and stolen her. As I continued to walk around and look, I remembered that I had given her a plastic dome-shaped doghouse to help her get shade on very sunny days. She was a pink pig with very fair skin, and she could easily get sunburned. I thought maybe I should look inside.

Oh boy! To my great relief, she was inside there sleeping soundly. Of course, I yelled, "Ester!" When I saw her, she woke up and came right outside. I knelt down to give her a good belly rub, which is one of her very favorite things. As I began to rub her, she flopped over onto her side and threw her head back in delight. Every time I do this, I cannot help but laugh because she is so incredibly cute.

As I went to stand back up, I was *prompted* to look inside her doghouse. The shape of her doghouse was curved, so it's hard to see directly inside of it. I had a strong *gut feeling* to look all the way inside. I couldn't believe what I found deep inside of her doghouse! It was a large pile of eggs! My mouth dropped open in disbelief. I knew that Ester had made friends with the chickens, but I also knew that she loved to eat eggs. I had made it a habit to give her all of the eggs on my farm that I had doubts about their freshness. She loved it when I would give her eggs. They were her favorite treats. As I sat there in disbelief, I then saw the mama chicken walk into Ester's doghouse and climb up on top of that pile of eggs. She wiggled around, nestling them, and turning them, and positioning them just right into the position she wanted. Then she fluffed out her wings and gently closed her eyes. Then I watched as Ester went back into her doghouse following that chicken and positioned herself at the front door of that doghouse. She also wiggled around a little as if to find her comfortable position, then she put her head down, and just looked up at me. I reached down and rubbed the little spot on her head right above her snout, and I told her that I loved her.

As I rubbed her, it occurred to me that she was actually guarding this pile of eggs and the mama chicken!

How could this be I thought.

Ester absolutely loves eggs. She will gobble them up as fast as she can if given a chance.

"What am I witnessing here!"

Somehow, Ester knows that there are baby chicks inside these eggs. How did the chicken come to know that she could actually trust Ester and lay her eggs in Ester's doghouse? I knew that I was witnessing something phenomenal. I also knew that I could have so easily missed this moment. It was something in plain sight, but I could have missed it if I had been too busy in my own world focusing on my own thoughts or chores or even worries. I also knew that I could have easily missed the *prompting* to go look for Ester. The prompting had been a very gentle thought in my mind. I've had many thoughts and *promptings* before, and I wondered how many I had missed that could have led to other amazing moments. I was so impressed with the level of kindness and awareness that Ester had toward these eggs and their mama.

I continued to check on Ester and her chicken and the eggs every day. After about a week, I went out to see them and all I saw were broken eggshells inside her doghouse. Ester, the chicken, and her babies were nowhere to be found! I was worried. I thought maybe Ester figured out that they were her favorite delicious eggs that she liked to eat and that maybe she succumbed to temptation.

Oh well, I thought. *Animals will be animals. That's what they do.*

I decided to go along as usual and check and feed all the other animals. To my great surprise, I found Ester with that same mama chicken. Ester was surrounded by twelve tiny, little chicks! I threw some chicken food down on the ground, and Ester, the mama, and her chicks all gathered around each other and ate together. Ester was so very gentle with her little friends. The babies would come right up next to her snout to get some food, and Ester would very gently nibble the food so as to not take any away from them. I noticed that when I had tossed out some of the chicken scratch food, some landed on top of Ester's back. All of a sudden, one of the baby chicks jumped right up on top of Ester's back and began to eat the little morsels of food. Ester stayed very, very still and continued to eat as she had been doing. There was so much peace in this moment.

I had been so amazed at Ester just being able to "know" to guard the eggs, but now it had been taken to a deeper level. It was as if she had been there when they were born and let them become part of her family. She was so kind and loving. This is something pigs are not naturally known for. They tend to eat newborns of any species. I sat and just watched her, remembering that she was such an overcomer of her own challenges, and now she was extending love to these tiny creatures. I watched them eat all of their breakfast.

Then Ester decided to lay down for a nap. The mama chicken sat close to her, and all of the babies ran to get underneath her. As they each made their way underneath the mama's plump feathers, one particular baby chick was struggling. This baby chick seemed to get turned around and started walking toward Ester and pressed up against her side instead. As I looked closer at that baby chick, I absolutely could not believe my eyes! That little baby chick had been born with deformed legs just like Ester had been! This little chick stayed close to Ester and nestled right up against her side, right behind her front right leg against her abdomen. It was like a little pocket for the baby chick. Ester did not make even one small move. She remained very still and closed her eyes. The baby chick then dropped her head and closed her eyes too. I tried to stay very still too so as not to disturb this moment. I couldn't help but breathe deep, and I could feel my heart beating inside my chest.

I began to think how Ester's little chicken and egg adventure had continued on and on into something that I could never have imagined. My little potbellied pig who already inspired so many people had found a way to extend so much love and compassion beyond what I ever thought a pig was capable of. We can learn so much from our animal friends if we will take a little time to really look and listen. I could have so easily missed all of these amazing moments if I had not paid attention to the *promptings* or *gut feelings*. I was so happy that I had been able to hear them. I wanted to have more and more opportunities to do this, and I wanted to learn so much more. I was so very thankful for even being able to witness this. It was such a gift. I knew that I had to share Ester's story to everyone that I knew. It has such meaning in so many ways, and maybe by sharing it, someone might grow in their own compassion to help others too and just maybe will also learn to hear the *promptings*.

Gecko Surgery

Many years ago on one very warm afternoon, I was home working in the garden while my two little girls played in the dirt beside me. They were ages five and three. This was a happy time in my life, and the three of us loved being together out in the sunshine. We planted lots of vegetables like tomatoes, cucumbers, sweet potatoes, and really tall, bright-yellow sunflowers. Every day in the late afternoon, we would come inside covered in dirt, talking about what we had done in the garden.

This particular afternoon, as we walked into the house, I went to the kitchen window to wash my hands, so I could start dinner. When I looked outside the window, I saw the flypaper that I had hung over the sink to catch the summer flies that were starting to come to my plants. What caught my attention was a small green gecko attached to the flypaper. He was stuck. Very stuck. All the way from his chin to his tail.

"Oh no!" I yelled.

The girls came running to me. I showed them the little gecko. I remember feeling very sad for him, and I knew that this was a terrible way to die; I didn't want him to. I shared with the girls what I was feeling and that I wanted to save him. I had a strong prompting to save him. They immediately had the same compassion. It doesn't take much to teach kids to have love and compassion. They began to beg me to get him off the sticky paper. I had no idea how that could even be accomplished. I reached up and cut the paper and carried him down gently to the kitchen floor. We could see his tiny eyes looking back at us.

My girls both said, "He must be so scared. What if he has a family waiting for him at home?"

Their compassion continued to grow for this little fellow. Then they asked me to pray for him. After we prayed, I focused on what to use to pry him off. I found a plastic butter knife. I knew I needed to try to separate him from the terrible sticky flypaper. I also got some Vaseline, thinking it would reduce the stickiness on his little body once we got him loose.

I began with his hands. I didn't want to start with his head and have something tragic happen. I gently pried one finger off at a time. I could not believe how tiny his little fingers were. My girls were determined. They sat right there on the kitchen floor not moving at all and helped to hold each little hand up as I got them unstuck. This process went very, very slowly. We finally got his little head and belly loose. As each part was loosened, I had the girls place a small piece of cardboard underneath him after rubbing the Vaseline on him. We lost a few fingers and toes and even the tip of his tail, but after more than three hours, he was finally freed. I couldn't believe that we had actually done it.

I grabbed some fish food and two tiny bottle caps to put the food and some water in. We covered him with extra Vaseline, so he could walk without sticking to the floor. He lived in our kitchen for a few days before finding his way outside. My neck, shoulders, and back were so sore from sitting hunched over on the floor, performing the "gecko surgery" that I laid back onto the floor in exhaustion. I could hear my girls talking to each other, laughing and cheering for the little guy.

Then they said "Mom, God heard our prayer and helped us save the gecko. Let's say another prayer to thank Him."

I was so humbled by their little hearts of compassion and especially their love for God. I sat right up, and they both put their little hands together and said such a sweet prayer of thankfulness.

It may have seemed that we saved a gecko that day, but I was actually blessed to see God's love through the eyes of children. My children. I knew that God had revealed something to me during this.

I was reminded that God is here, and He hears our prayers, and He can even use children to remind us of this. I said a quiet prayer of thankfulness for this moment to see Him through my children and for His love. I thought back to the moment that I had the *prompting* to save that little gecko. I could have easily ignored it, and I would have totally missed this blessing with my children. My heart was so full.

The Power of a Gut Feeling

Since my late husband died more than a year and a half ago, I've been trying to find some kind of direction in my life. I've tried all kinds of things, like rebuilding my aquaponics, getting into milking my goats again, going back to school, etc., and now I'm exploring my very long dream to participate in an open water swim event in the ocean. I've been able to practice in the ocean at least one to two times a week, and I've slowly been able to build up my confidence as well as my endurance.

When I'm in the water, I feel kind of *free*. Free mainly from worry, sadness, and grief. I see beautiful multicolored tropical fish all around me. It's also a place where I can hear my thoughts and I think even God sometimes. It's that quiet voice that comes. I'm trying to recognize it more. I also can hear what I call *promptings* or *gut feelings* that I know come from somewhere else. Personally, I feel it's from God. I know that if I listen, really listen, and tune in, it will guide me, teach me along this crazy thing called life.

Anyway, I absolutely love my time swimming in the ocean. This is why what I'm about to share may seem so peculiar.

One early, somewhat overcast morning, I headed for the beach with every intention of swimming like I've been doing for several months. As soon as I got ready to head down toward the beach, I felt a strong *prompting*. The *prompting* was "Do not go swimming in the ocean today." At first, I thought it was odd, and I tried to ignore it. I couldn't ignore it. The prompting kept coming to me. Again, I heard, "Do not go swimming in the ocean today." I actually could almost feel as if I was being stopped from going. So I decided to follow the *prompting*.

The next day, I woke up and wanted to try again. I did not have that same prompting. So I got dressed and off I went to my same favorite place that I always swam laps at. As I was getting my swim gear together on the shore, I couldn't help but overhear two ladies talking. It's what they were talking about that caught my full attention. They were talking about something that had happened yesterday here in the water, and they sounded very concerned. I had to know more. I walked closer to them and politely interrupted.

"May I please ask you what happened yesterday that you are talking about?"

The lady smiled but hesitated.

"Please tell me," I said.

She lowered her voice and almost whispered, "There was a shark here very close to the shore, but he's not here today!"

My heart literally skipped a beat. My *prompting* was right! Oh my gosh!

She said, "I don't want anyone else to hear me, so they don't get scared."

I tried to act very calm as I thanked her and walked toward the water. I wanted to get in the water, but I was feeling a little scared. As I stood in the shallow water fixing my goggle straps, I seriously pondered what had just happened and then I pondered even getting back in the water at all.

I could hear another *prompting*. "Don't let fear consume you, face it."

So I decided that I would get into the water, but I would stay closer to the shore today. I dove right in as I always did, and I swam a few laps, keeping the distance of my laps short and closer to the shore. I found myself swimming slower and paying more attention to my surroundings. As I swam, I just kept rethinking about the promptings that I had, telling me not to swim yesterday and then the "chance coincidence" of hearing that lady talk about the shark sighting yesterday right where I would have been swimming yesterday! I was beyond thankful for the prompting and that I had actually listened to it.

Several days have passed since I learned about that shark sighting in the same place that I've been swimming to train for my open water swim meet. I needed to get back into the water to keep up with my training, but I continued to find excuses not to go. I didn't want to admit it to myself or to anyone else, but I was scared. I didn't want to be scared, but I knew that I was. I also knew that If I didn't get back into the water soon, that I would probably just give in to my fear and give up on my dream. So I made myself go down to the beach.

As I entered the water, I put my goggles on, and I ducked down under the water. As soon as my head was underwater, I had a memory flash of a dream that I had the night before. The vision of my dream was so strong. I had dreamed about swimming in the ocean, and a dolphin swam straight up to me and looked at me. In my dream, I could sense that she wanted me to follow her out in the deep water. I remembered feeling peaceful and happy in my dream. I began to do my swim training and made it to the third buoy like I've been doing each swim session. This is the place where I get stuck because I have a hesitation to go out into the very deep. I tried to keep the thought of the shark sighting out of my head. I turned around and swam back and forth, staying close to the shore to at least increase my endurance. After about an hour and a half, I felt a bit tired, so I got out and headed for the shore. I was feeling thankful that I at least had gotten back into the water.

As I was heading to the outside shower to rinse off, the guy ahead of me said, "Hey, did you see the dolphins?"

I told him that I had not.

He said, "You've got to go back in and see them!"

Hmm, should I? I thought.

I made my way back to the shore. Even though I've had a life-long dream to participate in an open water swim event, to actually see dolphins in their own environment in the ocean has been a deep passion that surpassed any other dream that I have ever had.

Should I try to go back out in the water? I thought.

I could see snorkelers and a small boat far out in the water.

"Why not?" I said to myself.

So off I went. As I got to the third buoy, I just kept going. I headed for the deep water without any hesitation. I didn't even think about the recent shark sighting. As I continued to swim, I began to wonder if I would see any dolphins. I was hoping that I could get out there before they decided to swim away.

I said a little prayer deep in my heart, "Please, God, let me see at least one dolphin, please!"

I finally reached the area with the other snorkelers, so I stopped swimming and began to just tread water.

Again, I said, "Please, God, let me just see one dolphin."

Then I remembered that dolphins are very perceptive, so I sent them a mental message too. It was something like, "Please come so that I can see you!" I was hoping to see them, but it was so beautiful that I was just happy to be there. At that moment, I decided to look under the water. All I could see was beautiful blue-green water. It was so peaceful, so I just floated there for a few seconds.

Then all of a sudden…out of the corner of my eye…I could see something. As I stared at it, I barely could believe what I saw! Not one…but many dolphins were swimming right underneath me! I tried to count them as they took my breath away! I lifted my head to get a breath of air, and I could see dolphins above the water too! There were so many of them! They seemed to be circling me. I went back under the water, and I saw so many dolphins swimming underneath me then in front of me and behind me! There were so many of them that I couldn't even count them! Everywhere I looked, there were dolphins! My heart felt overwhelmed with joy and thanksgiving. I just stayed very, very still. I knew how important it was to not interact with them at all. It is vital to allow these animals to be safe in their own environment. I just couldn't believe that I was in the same water where dolphins were swimming. I honestly didn't think that

I would see even one dolphin. I looked at the other snorkeler and asked him how many dolphins were around us. He said at least fifty!

I had asked God to see one dolphin and He gave me fifty! I knew that I knew that this was a gift just for me. I spent the next two hours in total awe watching them from afar. They continued to swim away and then would come back. It felt so surreal. I wanted to remember every moment. After a while, I headed back toward the shore.

As I got to the third buoy, I realized just how far I had actually swum out into the deep. I had done it! I had actually gone past the third buoy with no hesitation and no fear. Then I remembered my dream again. What are the chances that I just had a dream about a dolphin trying to get me to swim out into the deep and then the very next day actually getting to do just that?

I knew deep in my soul that it had been a *prompting* or a *gut feeling* moment that had prevented me from getting in the water with the shark, and it had also helped to guide me back into the water when it was safe leading me to this moment. As I swam back to shore, I began to put all the pieces or steps together in my mind. I had been trying to overcome a "hesitation" to go out into the very deep ocean water. I had a lifelong passion to actually see dolphins and I had a dream about a dolphin actually encouraging me to follow her out into the deep. The man at the outdoor showers told me about the dolphins in the water, and then I felt the *prompting* to go back out into the water to take a chance. I had also asked God to please let me see just one dolphin, and I even tried to send a mental message to the dolphins themselves! I asked to see one dolphin, and I got to see at least fifty! Also, I was able to overcome my fear of swimming past the third buoy into the deep, so I can compete in the open water swim event!

I swam back to shore with a full and overflowing heart! I believe that this day may have been one of the best days of my life!

Disclaimer: I had this adventure before a new law became in effect here in Hawaii, which forbids anyone to intentionally try to swim with dolphins. I fully support the importance of honoring the safety and well-being of dolphins.

Operation Save Baby Catfish

I was so excited to have new baby catfish and tilapia! I was rebuilding my aquaponics systems, and I was heading to my friend's house to buy three buckets of baby fish. He didn't live too far from me, so I didn't think that I needed to bring any aeration. When we got to my friend's house, he had all the fish ready for us. He even gave me twenty-five extra baby catfish! I was beyond excited. I loved aquaponics because it included the amazing symbiotic connection of plants and fish. I loved learning how the fish helped the plants grow, and likewise, the plants helped the fish. I especially loved learning about the care of fish and even how to breed them. I was fascinated!

My daughter and her husband, as well as my late husband came with me. After we picked up the fish, everyone was hungry, and they really wanted to go eat lunch. I was a bit worried about the fish and knew that they couldn't be in the buckets for too long because I had not brought any aeration. I was persuaded to stop for a quick sandwich. While I was sitting in the restaurant, I kept thinking about the fish. We had only planned to be in there for just a short time. Well, as things usually go, we got distracted and interrupted. It even took longer than we had expected to get our order. We even had a man come up to us and offer us a huge amount of freshly harvested sweet potatoes that he had been unable to sell at the farmer's market. He passed out bags to everyone in the restaurant to collect as many sweet potatoes as we could. I was distracted by this, but I kept having this sinking feeling in the pit of my stomach.

At first, I thought this was just a sore stomach but then I began to have a bad *gut feeling*. There were so many distractions during lunch that I had actually forgotten about the fish! As we were collecting the sweet potatoes, all of sudden, I remembered!

"Oh no!" I yelled. I yelled so loudly that it scared the nice farmer!

As I yelled, my daughter said, "Oh, Mom! We forgot about the fish!"

We both raced over to our truck. I soon found out why I had a sick feeling in my stomach. All the fish were at the top of the bucket, gasping for air! I knew they were in real trouble. I had learned enough about fish through my own trial-and-error lessons that when fish get in this position, they have a very short amount of time to survive, and they may be beyond the point of saving. We needed to give them air, and we needed to do it immediately. We had no way to provide aeration. We were at least fifteen to twenty minutes away from any type of store that could possibly sell fish supplies, especially a portable aerator.

I had to think fast. Right at the same time, my daughter and I looked at each other. Her eyes were wide and big and so were mine! We were thinking the same thing!

Almost simultaneously, we ran back into the restaurant as we were talking at the same time, saying, "We gotta get some straws!"

As we raced to the cashier, we quickly asked for two straws and raced back to the truck. We both jumped into the bed of the truck, and without any hesitation, we put the straws into the water and began to blow air into the water! The only problem was we had four buckets, and there were only two of us, so we had to take turns blowing into all the buckets. My late husband came walking around to the back of the truck and looked at us in amazement! He hadn't known that there was even a problem.

As I looked at him, he just smiled while shaking his head and said, "There you go again, trying to save the world and all the creatures. This is why I call you Mother Theresa!"

I stopped for just a moment and told him we need to get to the store quickly for the portable aeration! He began to drive us as quickly and safely as he could, all the while my daughter and I were in the back of the truck blowing air constantly into the water with our straws while trying to keep the water and fish from sloshing out all over the place.

When we finally got to the store, I knew I had to be the one to go inside and get it because I knew the urgency, and I knew I would be the fastest to get in and out of the store. I needed someone to take my place, and I needed to find a way to give my daughter a break because she seemed to be on the brink of hyperventilation.

I remember thinking, *There's got to be a better way to save them! I don't know how much longer we can blow air through these straws!*

My late husband and my son-in-law tried to take over, but they had a hard time. I think my son-in-law accidentally swallowed some of the water! Poor thing! At least they bought me some time to try to find the aerator pump. I ran into the Target store. I headed for the pet section. I quickly ran right up to one of the workers and asked for help. I was talking so fast, trying desperately to explain my urgent situation. She just stared back at me. I can only imagine what she must have been thinking. After I repeated my story a few times, she got it! Then she started rushing around the store, quickly trying to help me too! She found the very last aeration pump in the whole store.

Then she said, "You need batteries!"

She grabbed the aeration pump and quickly determined what size batteries were required, and she actually ran to the front of the store and found them for me! Then she helped me find the shortest checkout line. Of course, the person in front of me had a problem that slowed us down. I think it was a problem with his debit card or something, so it was taking longer than it should have to move up in line. I began fidgeting and sidestepping back and forth all the while asking for help quietly in my heart for those helpless little fish. I was getting really worried. I saw the worker who had just helped me, and she began to pace back and forth too! It was as if she was worried for them also. I could see her gaze, and it was tracking all of the checkout lines as if maybe to find a shorter line for me. I was hoping that she could find one. Soon, she came up to me and ushered me to a different cashier that had just opened up.

Whew! I thought.

I was finally heading out the door, and I ran to the truck while ripping the plastic off the packaging.

I yelled to my family, "I got it!"

I struggled to put the batteries in it. Sweat poured into my eyes. I couldn't even see how to put the batteries in correctly. My hands were shaking.

My late husband reached over and took all of it and said, "Let me help."

I gladly let him. I headed for the back of the truck. I hoped that I wasn't too late. All of the fish were back in that same position with all of their mouths at the top of the water, gasping for air. Was I too late? I jumped up into the back of the truck. I grabbed the straw to start blowing into the water again. Right then my late husband handed me the aeration pump. I quickly placed it into one of the buckets. Oh no! I realized that I only had one aeration pump but three buckets of fish! We still had to blow into the straws.

My late husband said, "Let's get these fish home so we can get them into the pond!"

My late husband and son-in-law jumped inside the truck, and we quickly began to leave the Target parking lot. My daughter and I were still in the back of the truck, trying desperately to save the fish by trying to alternate the aeration pump and blowing air into the water. All of a sudden, as I was blowing air into the water, I gazed into the bucket, and I looked at one of the fish. As crazy as it sounds, it was as if our eyes met. Right then I had a *prompting* or a *thought*. I described it as a "big download." I thought of how we are like these fish swimming in the water. We are okay for a while with our day-to-day routine lives, and we just go about our normal activities until something happens. That something could be a financial crisis, a health scare, death of a loved one, etc. Then we feel like we "run out of air." At that point, we need help! Some of us may feel like we are "losing air," and some of us may even look up and beg for help.

We don't realize that we had been breathing all this time underneath the water and to be thankful for the help and blessings and for the "air." It's usually when we feel like the air is running out that we desperately look up for help.

Then all of a sudden, my daughter and I had the same *thought* or *prompting*. We said it out loud at the same time!

"Let's take our cups and fill them up with water and then hold them above each bucket and pour the water back in."

It will create air bubbles for the fish! How easy! Why didn't we think of this earlier? We joyfully began. It worked, and it worked quickly! Soon, the fish began to go back to swimming under the water instead of gasping for air. They looked so peaceful. It reminded me of how we are loved and cared for by our Creator.

My daughter and I could finally relax knowing that all of the fish had been saved! Soon, we drove into our driveway, and we successfully got all the fish into the big pond. My late husband noticed that we were not "frantically" rushing to move the fish.

"What's going on? Did they all die?" he asked.

I smiled and said, "We got a *prompting*!"

He grabbed a chair and sat down. He smiled back at me and said, "Tell me all about it!"

He knew about my *promptings*, and he often would say, "You've got to write a book and share these messages or *promptings* with the world!"

About the Author

Kim Dawson Hodson is an occupational therapist, mother of six, grandmother of four, widow, author, farmer, and animal lover. She has lived on the Big Island of Hawaii for 32 years and has a little farm with miniature goats, chickens, dogs, cats, a rabbit, and two rescue potbellied pigs, and one rescue sheep. She is also back in school, getting her certification as an animal-assisted therapist. She has been on a long journey for the past seven years. This journey has been one of painful loss, almost insurmountable grief, coupled with healing and new self-discovery. The healing began when she started to listen to the subtle "promptings" or "gut feelings."

As she began to listen to these, she had a deep realization that they are truly a gift providing her with hope. She has had many adventures—large and small—ranging from life and death to saving an animal who is in trouble to witnessing the amazing birth of an animal on her farm. It's as if these "promptings" are bread crumbs to guide her through this thing called life. As she continued on this journey, she knew that she needed to share her true life miracle stories, so she began to write them down. As she started to write them, she began to learn even more about how to really "look" and "listen" to the "promptings" or "gut feelings." These signs are all around us. She has written this book to bring a message of hope to everyone who reads it, and maybe, just maybe, can learn to hear the "promptings" too.

Milton Keynes UK
Ingram Content Group UK Ltd.
UKHW051819041123
431882UK00010B/98